SELF PUBLISHING TO AMAZON KDP IN 2024

A BEGINNERS GUIDE TO SELLING E-BOOKS, AUDIOBOOKS & PAPERBACKS ON AMAZON, AUDIBLE & BEYOND

BRIAN CHESSON

Copyright © 2024 Brian Chesson

All rights reserved. No part of this publication may be reproduced, distributed or transmitted in any form or by any means, including photocopying, recording, or other electronic or mechanical methods, without the prior written permission of the publisher, except in the case of brief quotations embodied in critical reviews and certain other non-commercial uses permitted by copyright law.

Trademarked names appear throughout this book. Rather than use a trademark symbol with every occurrence of a trademarked name, names are used in an editorial fashion, with no intention of infringement of the respective owner's trademark. The information in this book is distributed on an "as is" basis, without warranty. Although every precaution has been taken in the preparation of this work, neither the author nor the publisher shall have any liability to any person or entity with respect to any loss or damage caused or alleged to be caused directly or indirectly by the information contained in this book.

CONTENTS

Introduction   v

1. Inception   1
2. Self Publishing vs Traditional Publishing   3
3. What to Publish   5
4. What Is a Keyword?   9
5. Pseudonyms   25
6. Book Ideation & Outlines   28
7. Writing Your First Book   38
8. The Editing Process   43
9. How to Format Your Book   45
10. Creating Your KDP Account   49
11. KDP Select   54
12. Formatting Your Book Files for Upload   58
13. Book Covers   61
14. Uploading Your eBook   72
15. Uploading Your Paperback   90
16. Audiobooks   95
17. Pricing Your Books   99
18. Marketing & Social Media   103
19. Amazon Ads for Authors   107
20. Conclusion   115
21. Case Study   118
22. Bonus: Midjourney   121
23. All Links   125

Thank you!   127

INTRODUCTION

Wouldn't it be great if I could help you transition from point A to point B in just a fraction of the usual time? I'm betting you'd appreciate that, and that's precisely why this book is so concise. Unlike traditional books that aim for an arbitrary 250 pages, often because that's what the publishers expect, this self-published gem isn't bound by those constraints. Many times, authors pad their work with unnecessary filler just to meet that page requirement.

I've taken a different route, choosing to pack this book with nothing but valuable content, allowing you to breeze through, absorb the essentials, and put what you've learned into action right away. By the time you finish reading, you'll see for yourself that a book doesn't have to be lengthy to be worthwhile. And when it's your turn to write a book, remember this lesson: deliver the substantial, essential content your readers are looking for, guide them swiftly to their destination as promised in your title, and leave out the rest.

You might be pondering, "Why is he laying all his cards on the table? What's the benefit for him?" Here's the straightforward answer: embracing an abundance mindset has proven far superior to succumbing to a scarcity mindset. Adopting a belief in limitless resources attracts more prosperity and opportunities into your life

—it's almost miraculous. Hence, my intention is to disseminate knowledge generously and extensively.

And now, a candid revelation: while this book is crafted for a global audience, it also serves as a heartfelt missive to my brother and cousin. The business strategy I'm about to unveil is exceptionally robust. I've ventured into numerous enterprises, yet I invariably return to this precious strategy. I've accumulated a treasure trove of insights over the years, and I'm ready to share that wealth of knowledge directly with you. So, prepare yourself for an exhilarating journey, maintain an open mind, and anticipate excitement at every juncture!

As we proceed, bear in mind two essential points: all financial figures are presented in US dollars, and for your utmost convenience, I've compiled all the links mentioned in this book on a single page at the end, ensuring easy access.

To anyone who doesn't know or hasn't used Chat yet, here is a quick summary.

ChatGPT is a language model, that is, a type of artificial intelligence (AI) model that is designed to understand and generate human language. It's a computer program that has been trained on vast amounts of text data from the Internet to learn the patterns, structure, and grammar of human languages. ChatGPT can be used for a wide range of natural language processing tasks, including answering questions, generating text, providing explanations, and more. To begin using Chat, go to the OpenAI website, which is the organization behind ChatGPT. The URL is beta.openai.com. I'll use "Chat" going forward for brevity.

1
INCEPTION

Visualize this scenario: It's 2019, and I'm flat-out broke after an epic, year-long European escapade. In dire need of funds, I find myself resorting to the ultimate source of income—watching YouTube videos. That's when I stumbled upon Stephan James, who was enthusiastically discussing Kindle Direct Publishing (KDP). The idea? Write a book, publish it on Amazon, and just like that, you've got passive income.

Curious but skeptical, I plunged into a marathon of YouTube videos, determined to expose this as just another online scam. To my surprise, these YouTubers presented a compelling case with sound logic. It made sense. So, I thought, "Why not give it a shot? The worst that can happen is I waste a bit of time."

Stephan James suggested starting with a topic you're thoroughly knowledgeable and passionate about. Fortunately, I had been actively involved in growing and selling Instagram accounts, so the information was still fresh in my mind. Energized, I sat down and churned out an impressive 10,000 words in just a week—that's 2,000 words a day, thanks to my ample free time (with the assistance of Chat GPT, such a feat is now achievable in just a single day!).

Once my masterpiece, *Instagram Mastery*, was complete, I took the DIY route, creating a cover on Canva and formatting the manuscript in Google Docs. With a mixture of excitement and nerves, I uploaded my work to KDP, eagerly awaiting the magic to unfold. And just like that, a day later, my eBook and paperback were live on Amazon, and I made my first sale, earning a grand total of $2 in royalties. It might not sound like much, but to me, it was proof that this was the real deal.

Emboldened by my success, I set an ambitious goal: earn $2,000 a month. It seemed daunting and I was prepared to write thousands of books to reach it. But as it turns out, I didn't need to. A mere couple dozen books later, I was consistently making $2,000 a month. Fast forward five years, and I'm now earning over $10,000 a month from my publishing ventures.

Here's a valuable insight: attaining a monthly income of $2,000 doesn't necessitate having an extensive collection of published books —not by a long shot. And now, dear friends, I am eager to unveil my strategies and approaches to navigating the publishing landscape, as if I were embarking on this journey from scratch. In the forthcoming chapters, I will commence by explaining the publishing process, delve into the pivotal role of keywords, among other critical elements, before eventually exploring how ChatGPT can significantly enhance and facilitate your writing endeavors. Brace yourselves, as we are about to delve comprehensively into the tactics and strategies that hold the potential to transform this aspiration into tangible reality.

2

SELF PUBLISHING VS TRADITIONAL PUBLISHING

Firstly, Why Self Publish?

Do you know how to navigate the maze of securing a traditional publishing deal? Yeah, that's a mystery to many, including myself. From tales I've heard, it's a massive undertaking that often leads authors to fall out of love with their own creation. And the financial rewards? They're pretty underwhelming. Authors typically pocket a mere 10% of their book's sales, only to later realize that the heavy lifting of promotion falls squarely on their own shoulders.

Enter Amazon, a game changer offering a much sweeter deal. They hand you 60% of the royalties for your paperback (minus printing costs) and a whopping 70% for your eBook sales. To put it in perspective: a $14.99 paperback nets you around $6, and a $2.99 eBook brings in about $2. (Quick side note: there's a small fee for large Kindle books to cover Amazon's digital storage costs. This means if your eBook is a hefty one, full of images, your royalty might take a slight hit).

Now, you might be thinking, "But traditional publishers cover book design and formatting!" Sure, they do, but trust me, it's not worth the trade-off. With self-publishing, you escape the clutches of publishing deadlines, giving you the freedom to work at your own pace, without anyone breathing down your neck.

And don't worry—I've got your back. In the chapters to come, I'll guide you through the process of finding and hiring top-notch designers, formatters, and all the other pros you'll need to make your book a hit.

Should You Put All Your Publishing Eggs In Amazon's Basket?

In a word, yes. Amazon dominates the book market, scooping up nearly half of all print book sales and a staggering 70% of eBook sales. And they're not just big in the US; they have a global reach, selling books in countries like Canada, the UK, Australia, Japan, Germany, Italy, and more. They're constantly expanding, too—I recently noticed they added Poland to the list. By being on Amazon, you're opening your book up to a worldwide audience. And the best part? You just upload your book and they handle everything else.

Still need convincing to stick with Amazon? Here's another reason, based on something I've learned over my years in business—the Pareto Principle, also known as the 80/20 rule. This principle suggests that around 80% of your results come from just 20% of your efforts. The exact ratio can vary—it could be 90/10 or 70/30—but the main idea is that a small portion of what you do leads to the majority of your results.

What this means for you is that you can make 80% of your potential income by doing just 20% of the work. In this case, the 20% of the work is uploading your book to Amazon and then moving onto the next one. Chasing after the remaining 20% of potential income would require an additional 80% of work, a trade-off that just doesn't make sense. The 80/20 rule is all about efficiency, helping you focus on what really makes a difference and avoiding the trap of diminishing returns.

3
WHAT TO PUBLISH

Books come in all shapes, sizes, and genres, and today we're diving into the four primary categories they tend to fall into: no content, low-content, fiction, and non-fiction.

No Content

Welcome to the realm of emptiness, a place of pure potential! No content books are like blank canvases, offering a space free from the constraints of predefined content. Think of them as your personal playground for expression, be it through words, drawings, or whatever your heart desires. Journals and notebooks are prime examples of this category.

Low-Content

Now, let's shift gears to low-content books, where the words are few, but the opportunities are plenty. These books serve as a conduit for activities such as journaling, coloring, and sketching. They are the silent companions to your creative process, with examples ranging from planners and coloring books to diaries.

Fiction

Fiction, the land of make-believe, is where stories are born from the boundless realms of imagination. These tales are not tethered to reality, allowing genres like romance, science fiction, and fantasy to flourish.

Non-Fiction

On the other end of the spectrum, we have non-fiction, a category grounded in facts, reality, and the pursuit of knowledge. This is where you'll find books on history, science, self-help, and more.

Deciding on Your Book's Category

In deciding the category for your book, I have delved into various types and found non-fiction works to be the most promising. No content and low-content books are enticing due to their ease of creation, providing a straightforward and rapid production process that is perfect for beginners. However, it is crucial to note that these categories are heavily saturated, posing a significant challenge to make your book stand out amongst the plethora. In regards to fiction books, they're harder to market and make less profits due to more sales of eBook compared to paperbacks.

To stay competitive in the realm of low-content, you'll likely price your books around the $6.99 mark, resulting in an estimated royalty of about $2 per book. This means you would need to sell approximately fifty copies just to reach $100 in earnings. Furthermore, it's important to be aware of the major players and veterans in this field. These industry giants possess extensive knowledge and resources, enabling them to potentially operate at a loss to attract customers for future gains, a strategy that can be overwhelming for newcomers to compete with.

Another critical aspect to consider is the limitations in revenue streams for low-content books. You cannot make eBook or audiobook formats, which restricts your potential income channels and hinders your overall profitability. All these factors combined paint a clear picture of the challenges and considerations involved in choosing the right book category, guiding you towards making an informed decision.

In the realm of fiction books, possessing exemplary writing skills is paramount. Unfortunately, I find myself lacking in this area. To address this, I opted to employ ghostwriters to generate some books on my behalf, which yielded fairly satisfactory results. However, it's crucial to note that depending on fiction ghostwriters makes you reliant on their availability. In the event of their departure, the task of locating another writer capable of emulating their unique style can prove to be quite a daunting challenge.

While you might employ ChatGPT to address this issue, it's important to also pay attention to the specific reading preferences of your intended audience, especially when it comes to fiction books. A clear trend emerges within this demographic, showing a strong predilection for eBooks as opposed to traditional paperbacks. This particular choice has direct repercussions on your potential earnings as an author, with eBooks typically generating around $2 in royalties per sale compared to the $5 or more you might earn from paperback sales.

Furthermore, the intricacies of utilizing keywords for promotional purposes present unique challenges in the realm of fiction. The process of accurately targeting and implementing keywords for fiction books requires a nuanced approach, something that we will delve deeper into in the next chapter. Understanding these aspects is key to effectively navigating the fiction book market and maximizing your success as an author.

It's important to state that non-fiction books cover a diverse array of genres, including cookbooks and travel guides. I would recommend against diving into these specific categories. The necessity for colored images in these types of books leads to significantly increased production costs, as sourcing high-quality color images tends to be expensive. Additionally, the printing expenses for color images surpass those for black and white, resulting in a situation where your overall costs escalate while your royalties experience a downturn.

Considering all these factors, I have determined that concentrating on non-fiction books, specifically those that do not necessitate the use of colored images, is the most practical and economically prudent path forward. This strategy aptly balances the quest for profitability with the goal of reducing superfluous costs. I trust that, upon reflection, and by the end of this book, you have reached a similar conclusion, recognizing the wisdom in this focused and efficient approach to publishing.

4
WHAT IS A KEYWORD?

Keywords: A Gateway to Visibility in Book Publishing

In the dynamic domain of book publishing, the significance of keywords cannot be overstated as they play a crucial role in shaping marketing strategies and enhancing the visibility of books. Keywords are essentially specific words or phrases meticulously selected to encapsulate the essence of your book's content. They serve as navigational beacons amidst the vast sea of available book titles, guiding potential readers towards books that align with their interests and preferences.

To put it in simple terms, think of a keyword as the exact phrase someone would enter into the Amazon search bar from their desktop or mobile device while on a quest to find a book. Picture a scenario where a friend, your parent, or grandparent is on the hunt for a new book on Amazon. The phrase they type into the search bar, that's your keyword. To provide some concrete examples, a keyword could be something like:

- Yoga for seniors
- Ketogenic diet for women

- Puppy training
- Gardening in a small backyard
- Jokes for kids

The common mistake many authors make is crafting a book and then wondering why it's not selling. One significant factor behind this is the absence of relevant keywords. Even the most excellent book will remain undiscovered if it can't be found. Hence, our approach should be different — we need to ensure people are actively searching for the keywords we're incorporating in our title even before we commence writing.

How To Find a Keyword?

When choosing the right keywords for your book, it's important to understand a few key terms that will help you categorize and define your subject matter more clearly.

First off, we have the "niche." A niche is a big category or area of interest that includes many smaller topics. It's like an umbrella covering more specific subjects. For example, "pet training" is a niche.

Next, inside a niche, we have "subniches." These are more focused areas within the bigger category. If "pet training" is our niche, then "cat training" would be a subniche.

Going even further, we find the "book topic." This is the most specific area within a subniche. It's the main subject of your book, and it's the main keyword you're writing about. An example could be "clicker training for cats" inside the "cat training" subniche.

To make it clearer, let's look at a couple of examples:

For books about animals:

- Big category: books about all kinds of animals
- Smaller category: books just about pets

- Even smaller: books just about cats
- Very specific: books about clicker training for shy Siamese cats

For cooking books:
- Big category: all cooking books
- Smaller category: books about food from different countries
- Even smaller: books about Italian food
- Very specific: books about making gluten-free, vegan Italian gnocchi

These examples show how you can start with a broad topic and narrow it down to something very specific. Understanding these different levels helps you to better target your audience and pick the right keywords for your book.

To identify relevant keywords, start by exploring the primary niches on Amazon. You can do this by searching "Amazon book best sellers lists" on Google and selecting the first link that comes up.

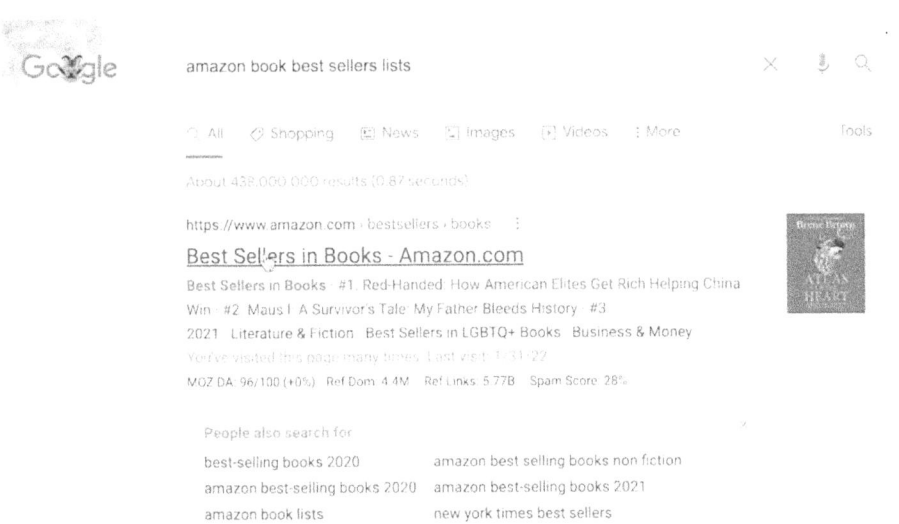

Upon arriving at the page, observe the assortment of categories listed on the left side. This collection encompasses a variety of subjects, including Arts & Photography, Business & Investing, Education & Reference, Health, Fitness & Dieting, and Self-Help, among others.

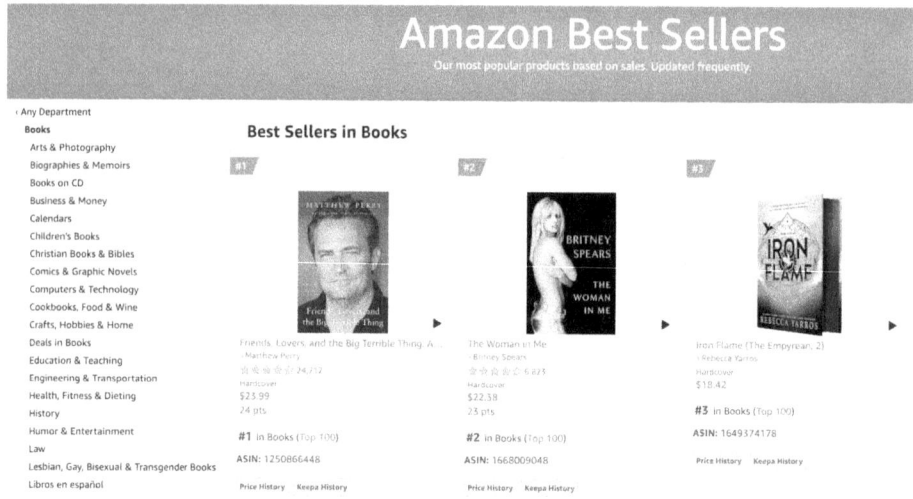

To refine our approach and enhance our chances of success, it's beneficial to steer clear of crafting a book within a main niche, given its expansive nature and intense competition. A more strategic move would be to dive into a specific category within a niche. Let's take the "Crafts, Hobbies & Home" category as an example. By clicking on this, we can delve into more detailed subcategories, such as "Crafts & Hobbies." From there, we can narrow down our focus even more, possibly landing on a niche like "Candlemaking." This method helps us pinpoint a more specific audience and reduce competition.

We've navigated through the categories as follows:

Crafts, Hobbies & Home (Niche) —> Crafts & Hobbies (Sub-niche) —> Candlemaking (Keyword)

As you delve into these specialized subjects, it may seem like you're entering a very niche market, and you might question the size of the potential audience for topics as precise as candle making. However, there's a popular saying in the business world: "The riches are in the niches." Even for such specific topics, the audience can be surprisingly substantial. By targeting these unique niches, you can face less competition, making them perfect opportunities to find your keywords and publish your book.

Here are some examples of keywords I have found for you:

- Meditation for teenagers
- Leadership for women
- Investing in real estate
- Cognitive behavioral therapy

- Budgeting for college students
- Facebook marketing
- Chess for beginners
- Ant keeping for beginners
- How to read sheet music
- Gut microbiome
- Vending machine business
- Off-grid living
- Public speaking for beginners
- Core workouts for seniors

Diving deeper into a niche can be achieved by tailoring the topic to specific audiences or skill levels. By adding phrases like "for beginners," "for experts," "for seniors," "for men," or "for women," you can narrow down your focus and cater to a particular group of people who are searching for content that is more relevant to their needs or interests.

So, with the example of "Ketogenic diet," you could indeed specialize further by creating content like:

- "Ketogenic diet for beginners" – which would cater to individuals who are new to this type of diet and need guidance on how to start.

- "Ketogenic diet for seniors" – which could address specific health considerations and dietary needs for older adults on a ketogenic diet.

- "Ketogenic diet for women over 50" – this would provide information tailored to meet the nutritional needs of women in this age group who are interested in the ketogenic diet.

When searching for effective keywords, it's essential to avoid overly broad or general terms, as they can make it difficult for potential readers to find your specific book among the vast sea of available titles. These are **not** keywords:

- Motivation
- Fitness
- Nutrition
- Music
- Adventures
- Relationships
- Why am I always tired
- Struggling to focus
- The power of now
- Secrets to wealth
- Oprah Winfrey
- Money magic
- Slim down fast for summer
- Science

When picking keywords for your book, it's crucial to stay away from terms that are too broad or general, like "self-help" or "exercise." Even though these words might seem relevant, they don't provide enough detail to help your book stand out. Additionally, using famous book titles or celebrity names can cause problems, as it could breach Amazon's rules.

Instead, focus on finding specific and unique keywords that directly relate to your book's content. This helps in attracting the right audience and avoids any potential issues with copyright or platform guidelines. For instance, rather than using a generic term like "exercise," a more targeted phrase like "low-impact exercises for seniors" could be more effective. This way, your book gets in front of the people most likely to be interested in it, while also adhering to necessary guidelines.

Finding Keywords with ChatGPT

This is the first instance in how we can use ChatGPT (I'll use Chat going forward for brevity) to help us in the book creation process. To anyone who doesn't know or hasn't used Chat yet, here is a quick summary.

ChatGPT is a language model, that is, a type of artificial intelligence (AI) model that is designed to understand and generate human language. It's a computer program that has been trained on vast amounts of text data from the Internet to learn the patterns, structure, and grammar of human languages. ChatGPT can be used for a wide range of natural language processing tasks, including answering questions, generating text, providing explanations, and more. To begin using Chat, go to the OpenAI website, which is the organization behind ChatGPT. The URL is https://beta.openai.com/.

Keywords used to take me days or weeks to find previously, but they can now be done in a few minutes. You can ask Chat a bunch of ways to find you keywords. Here are a few questions you can ask it:

1. I'm planning on writing a non-fiction book for Amazon. Give me a few specific keywords I can write the book on:
2. I would like to self-publish a non-fiction book on Amazon. I'm interested in the topic of Finance. Give me some options of what the book should be on:
3. I have expertise in the field of education. What are some specific subjects I could focus on for a non-fiction book to publish on Amazon?
4. I want to explore the field of technology in a non-fiction book for Amazon. What are some specific areas or trends that I could write about?

Engaging with Chat for inquiries of this nature can swiftly generate a plethora of keywords in mere minutes. Nevertheless, it's crucial to understand that this is merely the initial phase in the keyword research process. The subsequent and equally vital step involves evaluating the profitability and viability of each identified keyword.

Keyword Profitability

Delving into the profitability of keywords is imperative for your book's success. A key metric in this assessment is Amazon's Best Sellers Rank (BSR), a numerical value updated hourly to reflect sales performance.

A BSR of 1 places a book at the pinnacle of Amazon's bestseller list, whereas a BSR of 250,000 positions it significantly lower. Notably, BSR are different between eBooks and paperbacks. For profitability assessments, aim for keywords with a BSR of 100,000 or lower. To access a book's BSR, navigate to the Product Details section on its Amazon page.

Product details

ASIN : B0875Z2J69
Publisher : Independently published (April 14, 2020)
Language : English
Paperback : 132 pages
ISBN-13 : 979-8637201709
Item Weight : 7.8 ounces
Dimensions : 6 x 0.33 x 9 inches
Best Sellers Rank: #39,569 in Books (See Top 100 in Books)
  #1 in Candle Making (Books)
  #2 in Business of Art Reference
  #46 in Crafts & Hobbies Reference
Customer Reviews: 4.6 ☆☆☆☆☆   697 ratings

Useful Tools

For immediate visibility of Best Sellers Rank (BSR) directly on the Amazon search page, I advise utilizing the free Chrome extension plugin, 'DS Amazon Quick View.' Conduct a simple Google search, click on the first link, and follow the instructions for installation. This tool streamlines the process, allowing for efficient and rapid access to crucial BSR information right where you need it.

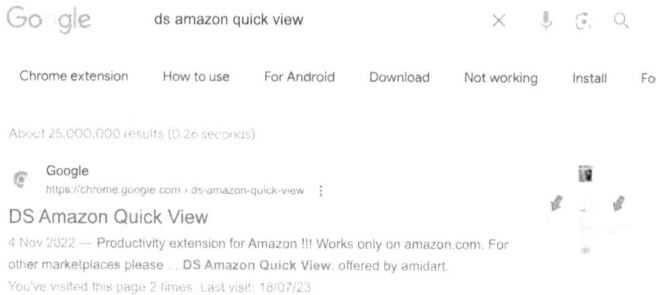

The display format will typically appear as follows:

KDSpy

I highly recommend incorporating KDSpy into your toolkit for keyword research and market analysis in the self-publishing domain. Although it comes with a price tag of $69 for a one-time payment, the value it adds to your workflow is substantial.

KDSpy operates as a Chrome extension, adeptly pulling data from the first page of Amazon search results and compiling it in an organized and accessible format. This tool stands out due to its capability to provide a thorough overview of competition and sales metrics for specific book topics, offering priceless insights that could otherwise be tedious and complex to gather manually.

The reality of the publishing industry is that, sometimes, making an initial investment can significantly enhance your potential for profit. KDSpy is one such investment that promises to pay dividends by cutting down research time and demystifying the intricacies of market trends and competition.

By utilizing KDSpy, you are equipping yourself with a powerful ally, designed to simplify your research process and enable more strategic and informed decisions. The tool transforms market analysis from a daunting challenge into a manageable task, helping you to navigate the self-publishing landscape with precision and confidence.

You'll find a link to purchase and download KDSpy at the back of this book. With KDSpy and DS Amazon Quick View at your disposal, you have the two essential tools required for comprehensive and effective keyword research.

Analyzing the Data

Utilizing "candle making" as our example keyword, the process of leveraging KDSpy begins by typing the phrase into Amazon's search bar. Following this, a click on the KDSpy Chrome extension initiates the tool's analytical functions. Within moments, KDSpy collates and presents a comprehensive array of data pertaining to all the books listed on the first page of the search results.

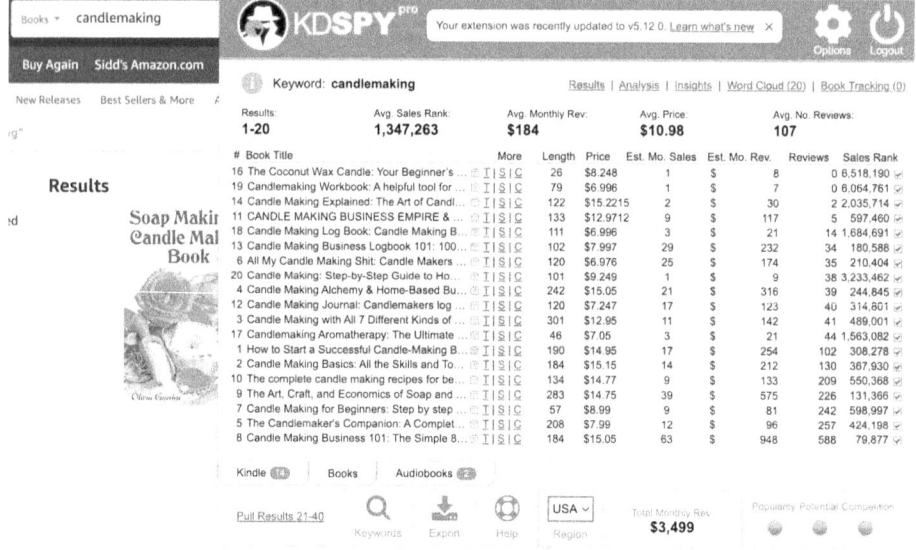

Let's focus on two important columns in the KDSpy report: "Estimated Monthly Revenue (Est. Mo. Rev.)" and "Reviews." It's crucial to understand that the revenue shown is what Amazon earns from selling the book, not the author's take-home pay. For instance, if a book shows $254 in revenue, this is Amazon's share, and the author typically gets about one-third of this amount, which would be roughly $84.

Now, let's look at books with 100 reviews or fewer. Why do we set this limit? It's because books that make money with fewer reviews show us that there's a good chance to succeed in this space. Even if our own book gets just a handful of reviews—around fifteen to thirty should do the trick for social proof—we should also be able to make the amount of money they're making.

By targeting books with fewer reviews, we are looking to enter a part of the market where there's not as much competition. This gives us a better shot at standing out and making good money with our book, especially if we can gather a few positive reviews to boost our credibility and help promote the book.

What to Look for

When we dive into the keyword "candle making" and focus on books with fewer than 100 reviews, we notice that the highest revenue is $316, translating to around $105 in profit for the author. What I generally look for is at least two other books bringing in similar revenue. This pattern gives me confidence that there's a strong demand for this topic. If I decide to write a book on "candle making," it suggests that there's a good market for it and a decent chance of making similar money as those books.

In this specific case, though, the demand for "candle making" isn't as high as I'd like. I found one book with 34 reviews making $232, and another with 102 reviews earning $254. So, if we decide to create an outstanding book on candle making, we could potentially earn somewhere between $232 and $316 in revenue. While this isn't a bad outcome, we need to weigh it against the effort required to create the book—it might not be the most profitable option out there. This is why it's a good idea to keep looking and consider other keywords.

A good target to aim for in your search would be a keyword where you can find three books, each with fewer than 100 reviews, making at least $500 in monthly revenue. While two books meeting this criteria might be acceptable, finding three or more is even better. It provides stronger evidence that a keyword is profitable, helping you feel more confident in your choice.

Conclusion

It is imperative to verify that the keyword you've chosen is incorporated within the title of your book. This practice is paramount, as it ensures your book appears in relevant search queries, maintaining both relevance and precision. To validate this, you can simply hover over the book title and scrutinize it in its entirety. Discovering the keyword nestled within the title is an encouraging indicator, signaling that you are navigating the path to success.

Moreover, conducting your keyword searches in an incognito browser window comes highly recommended. This tactic effectively eliminates any biases that may stem from your browser's stored data, offering you a clean slate of unbiased information. This, in turn, aids in rendering more accurate and reliable decisions based on authentic data.

To distill this down to its essence, the pivotal question you need to ask yourself is: "Are there at least three books with fewer than 100 reviews, each generating a minimum of $500 in revenue, and all incorporating the target keyword in their titles?" Meeting these criteria is a robust sign of a profitable niche. On the contrary, if these conditions are not met — and unless this is your initial publication — it might be prudent to reconsider proceeding. Venturing into a domain lacking demand or market interest can result in a futile exercise, squandering both time and resources, while failing to captivate your intended audience or generate the anticipated sales.

Chapter Summary

Understanding Keywords

1. Grasp the significance of keywords: Recognize keywords as pivotal words or phrases that encapsulate and categorize your book's theme, guiding readers to relevant titles.

2. Comprehend what constitutes a keyword: Realize that a keyword is what potential readers input into the Amazon search bar, ranging from specific subjects like "ketogenic diet for women" to "how to train my puppy."

Identifying Keywords

1. Break down categories: Delineate subjects from broad categories to highly specific topics to precisely target your intended readership.

- Broad category (e.g., cooking)

- Subcategory (e.g., international cuisine)

- Sub-subcategory (e.g., Italian cuisine)

- Specific topic (e.g., gluten-free hand-rolled gnocchi with vegan sauces)

2. Steer clear of vague terms: Avoid imprecise and overly broad terms such as "self-help" or "diet," which lack a niche focus.

3. Dive into Amazon's niches: Begin your exploration by searching "Amazon book best sellers lists," and delve deeper into specific categories, like "candlemaking."

4. Leverage Chat to swiftly generate a vast array of keywords within minutes.

Tools for Keyword Search

1. Opt for DS Amazon quick view: A Chrome extension to swiftly view BSR (Best Sellers Rank) directly on the Amazon search page.

2. Download KDSpy: A valuable Chrome extension for book data extraction, aiding in competition and sales analysis. Though it's a paid tool, it can be a time-saver and provide significant insights.

Analyzing Keyword Profitability

1. Understand BSR: Target keywords that have a BSR of 100,000 or less, as lower BSR signifies higher sales volume.

2. Look for keywords with reviews and revenue: Focus on keywords where books have less than 100 reviews but are generating revenue. Look for at least two or three books with similar revenue, ideally $500 or more.

3. Ensure keyword relevance: Make sure that the keyword is present in the book's title to ensure relevance.

4. Use incognito window for searches: To access unbiased information free from browser biases.

5. Evaluate the demand for a keyword: Ask yourself, "Are there at least three books with under 100 reviews, making at least $500 or more, and featuring the keyword in their titles?" If yes, proceed; if not, explore alternative keywords.

Be thoughtful in your choice of keywords. If a keyword doesn't match up to what's needed, it might not be worth your time. It's really important to pick a keyword that people are actually searching for, so you don't end up putting time and effort into something that won't draw in readers or sales.

5
PSEUDONYMS

Publishing on Amazon offers the flexibility to choose any name you wish, be it your actual name or a pseudonym.

Adopting different pen names for various genres is a strategic choice closely tied to the concept of branding. A well-established brand is crucial for achieving strong book sales and building a loyal readership. It creates a consistent image that attracts readers and keeps them coming back for more, eagerly awaiting your future works.

In my personal experience, I've carefully developed brands under specific pen names, focusing on language learning and personal finance. To maintain the credibility of each brand and prevent reader confusion, I make it a point to keep these niches separate.

Take Stephen King as an example. He's well-known for his captivating horror stories. If he were to start writing historical romance or create gardening guides, it would likely surprise his readers. This is a common reason many established authors choose to use multiple pen names. J.K. Rowling, celebrated for the Harry Potter series, released "The Cuckoo's Calling" under the pseudonym

Robert Galbraith. Using different pen names in this way helps authors clearly differentiate their work across various genres.

Handling multiple pen names on Amazon is a straightforward process, allowing authors to manage various aliases under one account seamlessly. However, it's imperative to avoid using the names of well-known authors, such as Stephen King, as your own pen name. Additionally, adopting titles like "Doctor" or "PhD" necessitates verification by Amazon to maintain authenticity and prevent misuse.

The decision to use multiple pen names might arise from a desire to explore different genres. For instance, an author may transition from writing finance books to self-help materials. I have personally navigated this scenario, choosing to establish a unique pen name and brand for each niche I've written in. This strategy proved beneficial, as I built email lists for each brand, allowing me to effectively communicate with previous customers and enhance the potential for repeat purchases when I release new books. Chapter 18 will provide more comprehensive information on utilizing emails for such purposes.

Choosing a pen name need not be a time-consuming process; often, a mere five minutes is sufficient to decide on a suitable alias. Select a name that feels right to you, and move forward with confidence. If you find yourself needing help, there are several resources available, including the pen name generator at https://blog.reedsy.com/pen-name-generator/. Additionally, ChatGPT can assist you in this task. You can provide a prompt such as: "I'm writing a book in the personal finance niche. Could you suggest five different pen names I could use?" This will guide ChatGPT to generate suitable and relevant pen names for your specific genre, making the process smoother and more tailored to your needs.

While I emphasize the benefits of building a brand, I also acknowledge that it's not an absolute necessity for achieving success with your books. I have personally authored several successful books without a specific focus on branding. However, I am particularly grateful for the brands I have developed under distinct pen names. They have significantly streamlined the process of selling future publications and garnering reviews, contributing positively to my ongoing authorial endeavors.

6
BOOK IDEATION & OUTLINES

Understanding that your first book might not bring in substantial revenue is important. It might even not generate any money at all. While this might sound discouraging, it's a common scenario for beginners, and it's better to have low expectations and end up surprised than to be let down. Rather than seeing this as a setback, treat it as a chance to quickly finish your first book and move on to the next ones, which could be more profitable. This mindset shift can make the journey less stressful and more focused on growth and future success.

When starting out with your first book, choosing a subject you are well-versed in is crucial. Take my experience as an example; my first book was about growing and selling Instagram accounts, a field I had a year's experience in and thoroughly understood. I recommend picking a topic you have knowledge of and are passionate about. This could be a hobby, like a musical instrument you play, a sport you participate in, or something related to your profession. Writing about your city and its unique aspects or exploring facets of your nationality could also make for interesting topics. The main goal is to find a subject that excites you and that you are familiar with, ensuring a more enjoyable and fluent writing process. While stumbling upon a keyword with profitable potential is a bonus, it's not a prerequisite—especially for your first book. This aspect can be honed and refined in future works once you have a published book under your belt.

To give you some inspiration, here is a list of book topics that I've seen successfully self-published on Amazon:

1. A Beginner's Guide to Running
2. The Digital Nomad's Handbook
3. The Ultimate Guide to Minimalist Living
4. Financial Fitness: A Guide to Wealth Building
5. The Mindful Entrepreneur: Building a Business with Purpose
6. Investing for Millennials: Building Wealth in Your 20s and 30s
7. The Science of Happiness: Achieving Lasting Joy
8. Growing Fruit Trees
9. The Parent's Guide to Raising Resilient Kids
10. Freelancing Success: A Roadmap to Financial Independence
11. Healthy Aging: Tips for a Fulfilling and Active Senior Life

I hope these examples help spark some ideas for your own book. ChatGPT can also assist you in brainstorming topics. Simply choose a subject you're interested in or know a lot about, and ask ChatGPT to suggest more ideas on that topic. For instance, if you're interested in finance, you could use the prompt: "I want to write a book about finances. Can you give me five specific topic ideas for the book?"

This is what it came up with:

1. Financial Independence Retire Early (FIRE) Strategies: How to Achieve Early Retirement

2. Investing for Beginners: A Step-by-Step Guide to Building Wealth
3. The Psychology of Money: Understanding Your Money Mindset for Financial Success
4. Budgeting Mastery: Create and Stick to a Financial Plan That Works
5. Real Estate Investing: From Rental Properties to Real Wealth

<u>Book Outlines</u>

Developing a clear and organized book outline is essential for a more efficient writing process. You can think of the outline as your book's table of contents, which acts as a guide for your content. Outlines can take different forms, from having a few long chapters to having many short ones. To give you an example, let's take a look at the table of contents from my book, *Instagram Mastery*:

1. Starting with the End Goal in Mind
2. Navigating Niche Selection
3. Selecting the Right Username
4. Crafting the Perfect Profile Picture
5. Utilizing Analytics Effectively
6. Optimizing Your Bio for Impact
7. Strategic Link Placement
8. Getting Your Instagram Journey Started
9. Crafting Compelling Content Ideas
10. Finding and Engaging with Relevant Accounts
11. Creating Eye-Catching Photos
12. Crafting the Perfect Video
13. Exploring Instagram Stories
14. Timing Your Posts for Success
15. Understanding Ideal Image Sizes
16. Maintaining Feed Consistency
17. Crafting Captivating Captions

18. Effective Hashtag Usage
19. Analyzing Instagram Accounts
20. Strategies for Growing Your Follower Base
21. Bots and Automation Tools
22. Building a Personal Connection
23. Contacting Other Accounts Strategically
24. Monetizing Your Instagram Presence
25. Advertising on Other Accounts
26. Exploring Additional Niche Opportunities

These chapters cover the top twenty-six questions I often got asked about Instagram. I turned each question into a chapter, providing thorough answers and information. You can use this method for your book too, focusing on popular questions or important topics related to your chosen field.

Below are various strategies you can use to create your book outline:

Mind Mapping

Start with a central idea or theme and branch out into subtopics or chapters.

Book title: Mastering Photography

- Subtopics:

- Understanding Your Camera
- Composition Techniques
- Lighting and Exposure
- Editing and Post-Processing
- Photography Genres (Portraits, Landscapes, etc.)
- Building a Photography Portfolio
- Monetizing Your Photography Skills

Chronological Sequence

When your book is centered around a historical sequence or a story that unfolds over time, a chronological arrangement of your outline can enhance clarity and provide a smooth reading experience.

Book title: Tracing the Roman Empire

- Chapter 1: The Roman Kingdom
- Chapter 2: The Roman Republic - The Early Days
- Chapter 3: The Height of the Roman Republic
- Chapter 4: The Transition to Empire
- Chapter 5: The Pax Romana - Rome's Golden Age
- Chapter 6: The Decline and Fall

Issue-Resolution Framework

Pinpoint the primary issues or hurdles that your book intends to tackle, and structure them as distinct sections or chapters. Within each section, you can then elaborate on resolutions, insights, or methods pertinent to that specific issue.

Book title: Navigating Relationship Challenges

- Section 1: Unraveling Communication Barriers

    - Chapter 1: The Role of Effective Communication
    - Chapter 2: Recognizing and Overcoming Communication Blocks

- Section 2: Strategies for Conflict Resolution

    - Chapter 3: Establishing Mutual Understanding
    - Chapter 4: Constructive Ways to Handle Disagreements

By adopting this structure, readers can gain a comprehensive understanding of the issues at hand and acquire practical strategies for resolution.

Comparison and Contrast Framework

In case your book revolves around the examination of different theories, viewpoints, or concepts, you can shape your outline to highlight these comparative aspects. Each chapter could concentrate on a particular pair or set of concepts, offering thorough analysis and examples to illuminate the differences and similarities.

Book title: Diets Unveiled - Analyzing Nutritional Regimes

- Chapter 1: Introduction to Nutritional Philosophies
- Chapter 2: Paleo vs. Vegan: Breaking Down the Basics
- Chapter 3: Ketogenic and Mediterranean Diets: A Side-by-Side Evaluation
- Chapter 4: Intermittent Fasting and Traditional 3-Meals-a-Day: A Comparative Study

This structure will enable readers to grasp the nuances between the different concepts or practices being discussed, providing them with a well-rounded perspective.

Subject-Based Structure

Segment your book based on extensive subjects or motifs, converting each one into a distinct section. Within every section, you can incorporate more precise subtopics or chapters to explore the topic in greater depth.

Book title: The Essentials of Gardening

- Section 1: Soil and Plant Nutrition

  - Chapter 1: Types of Soil and Their Properties

- Chapter 2: Essential Nutrients and Fertilizers

- Section 2: Plant Care and Maintenance

- Chapter 3: Pruning and Trimming Techniques
- Chapter 4: Pest Control and Disease Prevention

This format allows readers to navigate through the book based on their specific interests, providing a comprehensive and focused exploration of each theme.

Keep in mind, the strategies I've shown are just starting points, and there's plenty of room for creativity and customization according to your unique style and the specific requirements of your book. The main objective here is to cultivate a structured and systematic approach that streamlines your writing journey, ensuring that you produce a book that's not only coherent and captivating but also delivers a satisfying and enriching experience to your readers.

ChatGPT example

Chat makes it super easy to come up with an outline. It's as simple as asking it something like: "I plan to write a book titled *Investing for Beginners: A Step-by-Step Guide to Building Wealth*, can you create a table of contents for me?"

This is what it gave me:

Table of Contents

Introduction

- Why Investing Matters
- Who Should Read This Book
- How This Book Is Structured

Chapter 1: Understanding the Basics of Investing

- What Is Investing?

- Different Types of Investments
- Risk and Reward in Investing

Chapter 2: Setting Financial Goals
- The Importance of Clear Goals
- Short-Term vs. Long-Term Goals
- How Much Should You Save and Invest?

Chapter 3: Creating a Budget and Saving for Investment
- Building a Solid Financial Foundation
- Budgeting Techniques
- Strategies for Saving Money

Chapter 4: Building Your Investment Knowledge
- Essential Investment Terminology
- Where to Find Reliable Investment Information
- The Role of Research in Investment

Chapter 5: Types of Investments
- Stocks
- Bonds
- Mutual Funds
- Real Estate
- Commodities
- Alternative Investments

Chapter 6: Choosing the Right Investment Strategy
- Assessing Your Risk Tolerance
- Investment Strategies for Beginners
- Diversification: The Key to Managing Risk

Chapter 7: Getting Started with Stock Market Investing

- How to Open a Brokerage Account
- Buying Your First Stocks
- Monitoring Your Investments

Chapter 8: Exploring Bonds and Fixed-Income Investments

- What Are Bonds?
- How to Invest in Bonds
- Evaluating Bond Performance

Chapter 9: Mutual Funds and Exchange-Traded Funds (ETFs)

- Understanding Mutual Funds
- The Benefits of ETFs
- Building a Balanced Portfolio with Funds

Chapter 10: Real Estate and Property Investments

- Investing in Real Estate
- Types of Real Estate Investments
- Pros and Cons of Property Investments

Chapter 11: Monitoring and Adjusting Your Investment Portfolio

- Tracking Your Investments
- Rebalancing Your Portfolio
- Tax Considerations in Portfolio Management

Chapter 12: Common Investment Mistakes to Avoid

- Emotional Investing
- Chasing Hot Tips
- Neglecting Diversification

Chapter 13: Planning for Retirement and Long-Term Wealth

- Retirement Accounts (401(k), IRA, etc.)
- Creating a Retirement Investment Strategy
- Wealth Building Beyond Retirement

Conclusion

- Recap of Key Takeaways
- Your Next Steps in Investing

7

WRITING YOUR FIRST BOOK

Ensuring clarity in your book's topic is vital. If you manage to incorporate a keyword into the topic, that's a great bonus—it could potentially boost your book's visibility and sales. Nonetheless, if your topic doesn't involve a keyword, don't worry. View this as a learning experience, a chance to hone your writing skills and prepare for future projects.

Set your sights on producing a 10,000-word manuscript, targeting at least a daily output of 1,000 words across a ten-day timeframe (and remember, this is just the starting point—Chat should empower you to breeze through this swiftly!). The essence here is pace. Your primary goal is to finalize your book as fast as possible, enabling a quick and thorough learning of the writing journey, paving the way to your subsequent project. As you progress through each book, you'll accumulate practical knowledge, hone your craft, increase your writing speed, and become more adept at navigating the publishing process. This, in essence, is the straightforward reality and simplicity of the process.

When I started out, I took on the challenge of creating nine books, each with a word count of 10,000, spanning across three distinct niches. This extensive practice played a vital role in helping me master the necessary skills. Interestingly, one of these niches demonstrated potential for success, prompting me to channel my efforts there. To my delight, several of those books continue to generate sales, showcasing the enduring potential of this approach to publishing!

Keep this step simple and straightforward. Dive into the writing without worrying too much about spelling, grammar, or how your sentences are structured. Just let your ideas pour out onto the page. You can always come back later to edit and refine your work. What's important right now is to keep the words flowing and maintain your writing rhythm. Don't stop; just write.

In my daily routine, I found solace in visiting a beloved café each morning. Putting on my noise cancelling headphones, I would lose myself in the gentle strains of classical music from YouTube, all while enjoying a hot cup of black coffee. A Google Doc would be my canvas for the next ninety minutes, a space where my thoughts could freely transpire onto digital paper. In these moments of focus, I made it a point to avoid opening any other browser tabs, leaving me with two choices: revel in the quiet or harness the moment to craft words. This deliberate habit became my personal key to consistently hitting a word count of 2,000 each day.

Whether you have a full hour or just a brief thirty minutes to dedicate each day, don't be discouraged. Go into your writing sessions with focus and purpose, clearing away any distractions. This will enable you to steadily produce several hundred words every time. Remember, the most important thing is to keep up a consistent practice.

Using Chat

When employing Chat to expedite the process, rather than painstakingly writing out the entire book and then seeking Chat's assistance for revision, you can directly request pieces of the book based on your table of contents. It's crucial to remember that Chat cannot handle the creation of an entire book in one go; you must break it down into manageable parts. To illustrate, if we continue with our finance book example, instruct Chat to compose the initial section. Your request might be formulated as follows: "I'm writing a book on *Investing for Beginners: A Step-by-Step Guide to Building Wealth*, the first section is going to look like this, write it out in an informative and engaging manner:

Introduction

- Why Investing Matters
- Who Should Read This Book
- How This Book Is Structured"

This is what it came up with:

Introduction

Welcome to the world of investing, where the seeds of your financial future are sown and nurtured to help you achieve your dreams and secure your financial well-being. In this introductory section, we'll explore why investing matters, who should pick up this book, and how we've structured the content to guide you on your journey to financial empowerment.

Why Investing Matters

Investing is more than just a financial strategy; it's a key to unlocking your financial potential. It's the difference between merely saving money and making your money work for you. Whether you dream of retiring comfortably, buying a home, funding your child's education, or simply achieving financial peace of mind, investing is the vehicle that can take you there.

By putting your money to work in various investment opportunities, you can harness the power of compounding returns, which means your money earns money over time. This can accelerate your wealth-building journey and help you reach your financial goals faster than you might think possible.

Who Should Read This Book

This book is tailored for beginners who are taking their first steps into the world of investing. If you've ever felt overwhelmed by the jargon of financial markets, puzzled by the intricacies of stocks and bonds, or hesitant to start investing because you're afraid of making costly mistakes, then you're in the right place.

We've designed this book to be accessible to anyone with a desire to learn about investing, regardless of your prior knowledge or experience. Whether you're a recent graduate, a young professional, a parent looking to secure your family's future, or someone simply interested in growing your wealth, this guide will equip you with the fundamental knowledge and confidence needed to begin your investment journey.

How This Book Is Structured

To make your learning experience smooth and comprehensive, we've carefully structured this book into a series of chapters that will guide you step by step through the world of investing. Each chapter is designed to build on the knowledge gained from the previous one, ensuring that you have a solid foundation before moving on to more advanced concepts.

We'll start by laying the groundwork, explaining the basics of investing, and helping you define your financial goals. Then, we'll delve into various types of investments, strategies for building and managing your portfolio, and techniques for monitoring your progress. Along the way, we'll highlight common pitfalls to avoid and share practical tips to enhance your investing skills.

So, whether you're seeking to secure your retirement, save for a major life event, or simply grow your wealth, you're about to embark on a rewarding journey. By the end of this book, you'll have the knowledge and confidence to make informed investment decisions and take control of your financial future. Let's get started!

Next Step

By applying this approach to every section, you'll progressively construct your entire book. It breaks down the overwhelming task of writing a book into manageable parts, making the process less daunting and more achievable. Just keep going, section by section, and before you know it, you'll have a complete manuscript ready.

However, there are two crucial steps you need to take following this process. First, ensure the accuracy of all the information presented, particularly facts, as Chat may not always differentiate between true or false information found on the internet, necessitating a thorough fact-check. Second, verify that all the elements within your content seamlessly connect and flow well together.

8

THE EDITING PROCESS

Well done on hitting a major achievement—you've written your first 10,000 words or possibly even more! This is definitely something to celebrate, yet remember, there are a few more steps to take before your book is ready to be published.

Editing is a comprehensive process that goes beyond just checking for mistakes; it's about fine-tuning your entire manuscript to make sure it all fits together perfectly. This could mean moving around sections or entire chapters to make sure there's a clear and logical flow of ideas. Even though I usually start with an outline to guide me, I find that the editing stage often requires changes and reorganizing to achieve the best clarity and flow. It's important to remember that when you're writing and editing, nothing is final. Having the ability to edit, delete, or add content is a huge benefit of self-publishing, allowing you to continually improve your work.

A crucial strategy I've picked up is the effectiveness of vocalizing your text while editing. Simply scanning through the text might feel enough, but it's when you hear your words that hidden mistakes and awkward phrasing really stand out. Currently, there are plenty of free online resources where you can input your chapters and listen as they're read back to you. Using this method lets you truly hear your writing's rhythm, helping you spot and fix mistakes much more efficiently.

To elevate my editing game, I turn to Google Docs' "suggested edits" function. This first sweep picks out and helps fix straightforward mistakes and discrepancies. But for a more meticulous and exhaustive edit, Grammarly is my go-to. It goes above and beyond what typical word processors can do, catching a wider array of errors and providing useful recommendations. Merging these two editing powers, I'm able to bolster the textual quality and flow of my manuscript, aiming for a well-polished and seamless end result.

Remember, Chat has its flaws; it can produce text with odd phrasing or awkward sentence structures. Even though it can generate an entire manuscript, it doesn't mean the work is publish-ready. Readers are sharp—they will notice mistakes and leave unfavorable reviews. So, it's crucial to edit thoroughly. Run the text through Grammarly to catch and fix any errors it might highlight. This step is essential to ensure your work meets a high standard before publication.

9
HOW TO FORMAT YOUR BOOK

Fonts & Styles

When preparing your book for Amazon, choose fonts and styles that ensure a tidy and appealing presentation, especially on Kindle devices where formatting issues can be more noticeable. Stick to straightforward fonts like Calibri or Arial for the main text to guarantee clarity and ease of reading. When you need to emphasize certain text, make use of standard features like Bold and Italic, or bullet points for lists.

Make sure to format chapter titles with Heading 1 and use Subtitle for any subtitles. For paragraph spacing, I advise using the Open option, setting a twelve-point space between paragraphs to create a comfortable reading experience.

Utilizing white space between paragraphs is a popular strategy in self-publishing. It breaks up the text, making it easier on the eyes and preventing reader fatigue. To highlight specific parts of your text or add additional emphasis, don't hesitate to use Bold or Italic formatting. A font size between 10 and 12 points is usually best for ensuring your text is easy to read.

Page Breaks

Adding page breaks between chapters ensures a neat and professional layout for your book, especially when it's being read on Kindle devices or in print. To add a page break, position your cursor at the end of a chapter or section and press ctrl + enter (or command + return on a Mac). This will move the following text to a new page.

If you ever need to remove a page break, simply place your cursor at the beginning of the text on the new page and press backspace until the text moves back up to the previous page.

Page breaks help to mimic the feel of a traditional paper book, providing clear separation between different sections and chapters. To decide where to place your page breaks, you can look at a physical book for reference. Generally, the title page, author's name, copyright information, and table of contents each start on a new page. Sometimes, chapters also begin on new pages, with the content starting on the next page.

For the books I create, I insert a page break after the title and author's name, and then another after the copyright page. The table of contents is given its own page, followed by the introduction and each chapter. At the end of the book, I include a conclusion, an "About the Author" page, and a simple call-to-action encouraging readers to leave a review. This setup ensures a clean and user-friendly layout for both Kindle and paperback versions.

Book Size

Considering the dimensions of your book is an important step in the formatting process, particularly for non-fiction works. The most common sizes for such books are 5x8 inches (12.7x20.32 cm) and 6x9 inches (15.24x22.86 cm). These sizes ensure a balance between readability and portability.

- If your book is on the shorter side, with less than 30,000 words, the 5x8 inch size is a good option.

- For manuscripts that are approaching or exceed 30,000 words, the larger 6x9 inch size is typically more suitable.

Beyond these basic considerations, there are more advanced formatting concepts to be aware of, such as page margins and bleed. These are particularly important if you're planning to create a print version of your book.

While these advanced formatting details can seem daunting at first, you don't need to understand them right away, especially if you plan to hire a professional to handle them for you. However, if you do choose to tackle these aspects yourself, using software like Vellum can simplify the process significantly. Vellum provides user-friendly settings adjustments and a variety of tutorial videos on their site to help guide you through these more complex formatting considerations.

Has the Book Been Helpful So Far?

If this book has been of help to you, it stands a great chance of aiding others on their self-publishing journey as well. Your feedback is immensely valuable, and sharing your thoughts can make a significant difference. I kindly ask for just a moment of your time, merely thirty seconds, to leave a review and share your experience.

Your insights and opinions could very well light the way for someone else navigating the intricacies of self-publishing, helping them find clarity and direction. Simply scan the QR code provided here, and it will direct you straight to the Amazon page where you can easily leave your review. Your contribution is greatly appreciated, and you'll be playing a pivotal role in creating a community of support and knowledge-sharing. Thank you for considering this small act of kindness.

10

CREATING YOUR KDP ACCOUNT

Originally, KDP stood for "Kindle Direct Publishing," reflecting its exclusive focus on publishing books for the Kindle platform. Over time, though, the service expanded to include paperback and hardcover editions, broadening the scope of publishing options for authors. Despite this evolution, the name "KDP" has remained, becoming synonymous with Amazon's self-publishing services.

Now that your book is polished and ready for the world, the next step is setting up your KDP account. It's crucial to be aware of Amazon's terms and conditions in this process: they allow only one KDP account per individual. Creating multiple accounts can result in termination and a permanent ban from using KDP.

You have the option to use your existing Amazon shopping account to create your KDP account, or you can start fresh with a new email address. The choice is yours, but ensure you comply with Amazon's policies to maintain good standing on the platform.

To initiate the creation of your KDP account, navigate to kdp.amazon.com/signin and locate the prominent "Get Started" button situated at the top right corner of the page. Click on it to begin the process.

Setting up your KDP account is a detailed procedure that involves multiple steps, requiring you to provide extensive information. This includes vital personal and financial details such as your Social Security Number (necessary for tax purposes) and your bank account routing numbers (to facilitate the direct deposit of your monthly royalty earnings).

After diligently completing the registration process, you will gain access to the KDP dashboard. This hub is segmented into four main sections for easy navigation:

- **Bookshelf:** This is where your published and draft books are stored. You can also start new book projects from here.

- **Reports:** This section provides detailed analytics and earnings reports, helping you track your book sales and royalties.

- **Community:** Engage with other authors and find valuable resources in this community space.

- **Marketing:** Access promotional tools and options to boost the visibility and sales of your books.

Bookshelf

The Bookshelf is the designated space for uploading and accessing your books. To add a new title, click on the prominent yellow "+ Create" button. You will be presented with several options: Kindle eBook, Paperback, Hardcover, and Series. The Series option is particularly useful for linking books in a series, providing a seamless reading flow for the audience. In this book, we will primarily focus on Kindle eBook and Paperback, which will be explored in greater detail in chapters fourteen and fifteen.

Reports

The Reports section in your KDP account is for monitoring your earnings. Amazon introduced significant updates to this segment in late 2022, unveiling a variety of new tabs under the Reports tab. These include Dashboard, Orders, KENP Read (which stands for Kindle Edition Normalized Pages Read and reflects the page reads for books enrolled in Kindle Select; more details in the next chapter), Month-to-Date, Promotions, Pre-orders, and Royalties Estimator.

One of the greatest joys in self-publishing is witnessing the financial rewards of your hard work. Observing the sales, tracking the growth, and watching your royalties accumulate offers a sense of achievement and fulfillment. For Kindle eBooks, Amazon provides two royalty options: 35% and 70%. The 35% royalty rate is applicable worldwide, while the 70% rate is restricted to specific territories, including but not limited to the United States, United Kingdom, Australia. Various factors, including VAT, promotional pricing, and delivery costs, influence the calculation of your royalties.

When it comes to paperback books, Amazon retains 40% of the sales, leaving you with a 60% cut after the subtraction of printing expenses. Royalties are paid out two months following the month in which they were accrued, and a minimum balance of $100 is necessary for a payout. Typically, payments are made via direct deposit to your bank account on the final day of the month, though this can vary based on your country and bank. Although waiting for payment can be somewhat tedious, maintaining regular uploads and achieving consistent sales can lead to a steady increase in earnings over time.

Community

The Community tab in your KDP account serves as a hub for resources and support. Here, you'll find official Amazon announcements and forums that foster a sense of camaraderie among publishers. These platforms allow users to exchange tips, seek guidance, and share their publishing experiences. For those new to the community, navigating the forums might seem daunting at first. However, actively reading through the posts can prove to be an invaluable learning experience.

In addition to the forums, the Community tab provides access to the Amazon Help section, a comprehensive repository of information addressing a wide array of account-related questions. This section is packed with tutorials, user guides, and detailed articles that cover the intricacies of using the KDP platform.

Should you require personalized assistance, the "Contact Us" feature is readily available under the Help tab within the Community section. Clicking on this link guides you through a series of prompts, ensuring you have access to pertinent information before ultimately reaching out to Amazon's support team.

Marketing

The Marketing tab within your KDP account is a portal to a range of promotional resources tailored for your book's success.

KDP Select: Opting into KDP Select grants your eBooks exclusive distribution on Amazon for a ninety-day period, during which they become eligible for additional promotional opportunities and can earn revenue from the Kindle Unlimited and Kindle Owners' Lending Library programs.

Amazon Ads: This feature directs you to Amazon's advertising portal, where you can create and manage effective marketing campaigns to increase your book's visibility and drive sales.

Author Central: Manage your author profile and keep track of your books, sales ranks, and customer reviews from one centralized location.

A+ Content: Elevate your product detail pages with A+ content, incorporating images, text modules, and comparison tables to provide potential readers with a richer and more informative browsing experience.

Run a Price Promotion: Leverage the perks of KDP Select to organize Kindle Countdown Deals or Free Book Promotions. These promotional activities can be set up either directly from the Bookshelf page or within your book's individual listing.

Nominate your eBooks: Get involved in Amazon's special promotions and contests by nominating your eBooks for Kindle Deals, offering time-limited discounts, or for inclusion in Prime Reading, where selected eBooks are made available at no extra cost to Prime members.

11

KDP SELECT

What Is KDP Select?

KDP Select is a specialized ninety-day program exclusively for Kindle eBooks. Enrolling in this program allows you to gain the opportunity to reach a broader audience through Amazon and makes your book accessible to Kindle Unlimited subscribers. Kindle Unlimited is a subscription service from Amazon that allows its members to read as many books as they want from the program's catalog at no additional cost.

However, it is crucial to be aware of the commitments involved with KDP Select. Once you choose to enroll your eBook in this program, you are agreeing to distribute it exclusively through Amazon, and you cannot publish it on any other online platforms during the ninety-day period. While this exclusivity provides you with the full benefits of the Kindle ecosystem and potentially increases your reach and visibility, it also narrows your distribution options outside of Amazon.

In essence, KDP Select offers a trade-off between broader visibility on Amazon and the limitations of exclusive distribution.

KDP Select Benefits

KDP Select offers several advantages for authors. Firstly, authors earn money from Amazon every time their book is borrowed and read through the Kindle Unlimited program. Amazon puts aside a certain amount of money each month for the KDP Select Global Fund, which is then shared among authors based on the number of their borrowed and read books. While this can provide additional income, it's usually a modest amount.

Secondly, KDP Select provides access to Kindle Countdown Deals, allowing authors to temporarily reduce the price of their book. This creates a sense of urgency and can boost sales. For instance, a book usually priced at $6.99 could be discounted to $0.99. This discounting can run for up to five days within each ninety-day enrollment period.

Thirdly, authors can choose to make their eBook free for up to five days every ninety days, attracting even more readers. The Free Book Promotion tool lets authors offer their book for free to anyone on Amazon, not just Kindle Unlimited subscribers. Authors can run this promotion for up to five days consecutively or split it across multiple days. You also have the flexibility to cancel promotions if you change your mind.

I prefer running a two-day free promotion for my book, followed by another three-day free promotion about a month later, and I repeat this pattern in every ninety-day cycle. Doing this helps to boost the visibility of my book and attract more readers. It's great because when someone downloads my book during a free promotion and leaves a review, it counts as a "verified review." These verified reviews are more impactful than "unverified reviews," adding genuine value and credibility to my book.

A "verified review" on Amazon is a customer review that has been confirmed as a genuine purchase of the product being reviewed. It is marked with a "Verified Purchase" label, indicating that the reviewer bought the product through Amazon.

An "unverified review," on the other hand, is a review where the reviewer may not have purchased the product through Amazon or their purchase couldn't be verified by Amazon. Amazon allows anyone with an Amazon account to leave a review on a product page, whether they purchased the product through Amazon or not. Unverified reviews are not marked with a "Verified Purchase" label. This means that the reviewer might have obtained the product from a different source or did not make the purchase through Amazon, and as a result, Amazon cannot confirm their direct experience with the product.

Reviews are incredibly important. They act as social proof, showing potential readers that others have read and appreciated a book. This positive feedback makes a book more appealing, helps it stand out, and ultimately leads to increased popularity and sales. Ensuring that a book gets good reviews is a fundamental strategy to attract more readers and increase a book's success on Amazon.

Unverified review:

patrick

☆☆☆☆☆ **Keto diet resource**
Reviewed in the United States 🇺🇸 on July 14, 2023
Recipes are fairly easy to follow. Results are amazing if you follow them.

Helpful   Report

Verified review:

Yesica

☆☆☆☆☆ **Bought as a gift**
Reviewed in the United States 🇺🇸 on July 13, 2023
Verified Purchase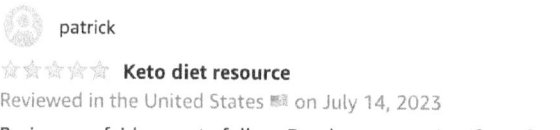
Very nice look.

Helpful   Report

My Thoughts

Enrolling in KDP Select seems like a smart choice to me. Even though I don't have solid proof, I strongly believe that Amazon gives more attention and shows books in this program to more people. This makes sense because it helps both Amazon and the authors.

I have also tried taking my books out of KDP Select to publish them on other platforms like Apple, Kobo, and Barnes & Noble through Draft2Digital. But, the money I made from that – around $100-$200 per month – was not worth the extra work it took.

This is a clear example of the 80/20 rule, where 20% of the efforts bring in 80% of the results. By keeping your eBooks in Amazon's KDP Select, you're likely to get more exposure and earn more, making it a more efficient use of your time and resources.

12

FORMATTING YOUR BOOK FILES FOR UPLOAD

There are four main ways to get your book files ready for Amazon: doing it yourself in Word, using Kindle Create, trying out Vellum, or hiring someone who specializes in formatting.

Formatting in Word

Once you've formatted your book's content to your liking, you can directly upload it to Amazon using the Web Page Filtered format (.DOCX). Choose "Save As" and pick where you want to save it on your computer. While this method is great for making quick edits and updates, it's a bit limited in terms of formatting options and might not give your book that polished look.

Using Kindle Create for Formatting

Kindle Create is a complimentary book formatting tool from Amazon, designed for both Kindle eBooks and paperbacks. Begin by downloading Kindle Create (you can easily find it by searching "Kindle Create download" on Google and selecting the first result). Next, upload your .DOCX book file into the software. Kindle

Create offers a variety of optional features, such as creating a clickable table of contents, and providing various formatting styles for chapter headings and subtitles. Take advantage of these tools, tweaking and refining them to suit your requirements before making your book available for publication.

Formatting in Vellum

Vellum is a popular book formatting software available at Vellum.com, favored by many authors for its comprehensive features. It provides users with advanced formatting options, including personalized drop caps, decorative flourishes, box sets, and tailored formatting for different platforms. While Vellum is not free, requiring a one-time payment of $199 at the time of writing this, it offers exceptional flexibility and customization options. This allows you to give your book a sleek, professional look that stands up to those published by major industry players.

Engaging a Professional Formatter

For those who feel daunted by the task of formatting, there's the option to bring a professional formatter on board from websites like Fiverr or Upwork. You can find a variety of formatting services available at various price levels on these platforms. It's important to carefully go through the feedback left by previous clients, read through the service offerings, and pay attention to how many revisions are included when choosing a professional to work with.

Preparing your book files for upload is an essential stage in self-publishing, and while it might seem daunting at first, it's a task that can be tackled either independently or with professional assistance. Personally, I've found immense value in using Vellum for this purpose. If you're serious about publishing and intend to do it on a long-term basis, dedicating time to learn and invest in Vellum is highly recommended. It streamlines the publishing process by cutting down the need for continuous back-and-forth with freelancers during the formatting stage. Additionally, it becomes a cost-effective option in the long haul. However, it's important to mention that Vellum is only available for Mac users, although PC users can access it via the cloud.

13

BOOK COVERS

The role of book covers in selling books on Amazon is incredibly vital. Despite the common saying not to judge a book by its cover, the reality is that potential buyers often make their initial decision based on the book's visual appeal. Given that customers don't have much else to base their decision on when browsing online, the cover becomes a significant factor. In this chapter, we will delve into several approaches to creating book covers that are apt for both Kindle and paperback formats. These include crafting your own covers using graphic design tools, employing a professional designer, or engaging a specialized design company to create a cover for you.

Before we dive into the different methods of creating book covers, it's crucial to grasp the essential elements of book covers on Amazon, particularly for Kindle eBooks. Amazon has laid out specific guidelines that must be followed. These include a recommended height/width ratio of 1.6:1 and a minimum image height of 2,500 pixels to ensure clarity on high-definition devices. The cover files should ideally be 2,560 x 1,600 pixels in dimensions, and the file size must not surpass 50MB. Importantly, ensure that your cover design steers clear of copyright infringement and avoid placing any pricing information or temporary promotional details directly on the cover.

Design Your Own Book Cover Using Graphic Design Software

Creating your book cover through graphic design software is a fitting choice if you have a knack for design or are open to acquiring the skills, particularly when you're working on one of your first books and are not anticipating substantial earnings from it. Adobe Photoshop and Canva.com stand out as two prevalent graphic design tools. My suggestion would be to give Canva a try, as it not only provides a user-friendly interface but also frequently comes with a free trial option. To help kickstart your design journey, you can take advantage of numerous tutorials available on YouTube that cover the fundamental aspects of image design, guiding you through the process of putting together your book cover.

Hire a Professional Designer

Opting for a professional designer is a wise decision if you aim to establish a thriving business in selling books. Platforms such as Fiverr and Upwork present seamless avenues to either advertise job openings or seek out freelancers who specialize in crafting book covers. These websites showcase portfolios and previous work samples, aiding you in identifying a designer who has a grasp on various genres and possesses the capability to draw in prospective readers. Simply input "book cover designer" in the search bar, and you'll be greeted with an extensive selection of freelancers to consider for your project.

Starting out, Fiverr can be a great platform to quickly find and hire a designer. You can scroll through various profiles, take a look at the artists' past work, and if you find a style that appeals to you and seems of good quality, you can proceed to hire them. Simply give them the details they need, and they can start working on your book cover. It's worth noting that some designers might offer their services at very low prices, like $5 per design. While this is budget-friendly, keep in mind that the quality might not always meet high standards. To start off, my recommendation would be to hire three or four different designers from this price range, see which aspects of their designs you like, and then choose one designer to incorporate those liked elements into a final cover design. With this approach, and an approximate investment of $20, you can end up with a stunning book cover.

When your business starts to flourish, upgrading to a committed designer who grasps your unique vision becomes vital. Upwork stands out as an ideal platform for such progression, facilitating direct and productive communication. With time, this enables the nurturing of a rapport with a particular designer tailored to meet your specific requirements. Speaking from my experience, I now have a dedicated designer on standby. A quick message is all it takes, and within a day or two, they respond with a top-notch, one-of-a-kind cover design. This is all thanks to the strong working relationship we've established. At present, my designer charges me $50 per cover.

Hire a Professional Design Company

If you opt to go with a professional design company, there are plenty to choose from that specialize in creating stunning book covers. One service that I personally recommend is 100 Covers. Their team of adept designers provides quality covers at an affordable rate of $100, and you can often snag a discount by doing a quick online search for "100 Covers discount code," potentially bringing the cost down to just $50. The company typically delivers within a one to two-week timeframe and offers the benefit of unlimited revisions. This means you can place your order as soon as you've settled on your book's topic and title. While you dedicate your time to writing, the design team works simultaneously on your cover. By the time your manuscript is complete, your professionally designed cover should be ready to go. This presents a smart, budget-friendly option, particularly if you're not quite ready to invest in developing design skills or hiring an individual professional just yet.

Paperback Covers

When it comes to creating a cover for a paperback book, remember that your cover file needs to be a single PDF image that includes the front cover, spine, and back cover. The dimensions of this image will vary based on the number of pages in your book and its trim size. To make this process easier, Amazon offers a handy Paperback file setup calculator and cover templates. All of these resources are freely available and can be found by visiting the following link: https://kdp.amazon.com/en_US/cover-calculator. This tool is essential in ensuring that your paperback cover meets Amazon's specifications and looks professional when printed.

Transforming an eBook cover into a paperback version can be both budget-friendly and straightforward. You have the opportunity to use platforms like Fiverr.com, where you can hire an individual to do the job for as little as $5. Alternatively, Canva.com offers a user-friendly option; you can download the necessary template and design the spine and back cover on your own. Opting for this do-it-yourself approach or utilizing cost-effective online services usually ends up being less expensive than hiring a professional designer or a design company.

Before establishing a relationship with my own designer, I discovered an effective method by using 100 Covers to produce the front cover at an affordable rate of $50. Subsequently, I took on the task of designing the spine and back cover myself. This strategy not only saved money but also precious time, minimizing the necessity for extensive communication on Fiverr and accelerating the overall process, leading to a smoother and quicker workflow.

Understanding What Makes an Excellent Book Cover

To truly grasp the subtleties of the book covers discussed in the upcoming sections, I invite you to scan the QR code found at the end of this book. By entering your information, you'll receive a vivid PDF directly to your inbox, providing a visual guide to help you comprehend the components that contribute to a top-selling book cover. Creating an eye-catching book cover is an intricate art, involving various elements. However, there are several key principles that consistently play important roles in the process:

1. Theme Consistency: Ensure that your cover visually represents the core message and genre of your book. It should act like a visual teaser of your story or content.

2. Title Clarity: Choose a font size that is big enough and a color palette that stands out, ensuring that your title is easily readable even at a quick glance or when viewed as a small thumbnail.

3. Professionalism: A sleek, polished cover communicates to potential readers that they are investing in a quality product. Never underestimate the impact of a good first impression.

4. Attention-Grabbing: This is the tricky part but it's also the most crucial. Your cover should be so compelling that it stops potential readers in their tracks, prompting them to click and learn more about your book. Achieving this is challenging, but it's essential for capturing interest in the competitive world of book selling.

Let's embark on an engaging exercise and attempt to unravel the mysteries behind these book covers, all while keeping their titles out of view:

Starting off with the cover on the left, what's your top speculation? Focus on the components present on the cover; what narrative do they appear to weave? Shifting to the one in the center, are you able to discern the kinds of food illustrated on the cover? Moving on to the cover on the right, what's your intuition saying? Proceed to the subsequent page to discover if your guesses hit the mark!

Even without a glimpse at the titles, you can likely form some informed assumptions about the first two covers. The one on the left teems with motifs related to honey, suggesting a probable connection to beekeeping or honey making. The middle cover, adorned with images of cookies and brownies, might lead you to deduce that it's either a cookbook or a guide to baking. The cover on the right, however, is more ambiguous. Its imagery doesn't clearly indicate a theme of finance, resulting in both the picture and title failing to communicate the book's content effectively, rendering it a less successful cover.

The complete titles for the book covers are as follows:

Beekeeping for Beginners: The New Complete Guide to Raise a Healthy and Thriving Beehive

100 Cookies: The Baking Book for Every Kitchen, with Classic Cookies, Novel Treats, Brownies, Bars, and More

Looking Ahead: Life, Family, Wealth And Business After 55

Let's go for another round. This time, I want you to compare the cover on the left with the one on the right. Decide which one captures your interest more effectively. Make your choice and then check below to see if you've made a good pick.

 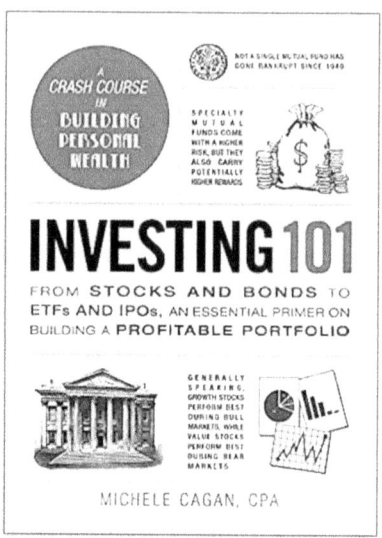

If you chose the cover on the right, you've got a good eye! Both books explore the realm of investing, yet it's the right cover that adeptly intertwines finance and investment imagery. Not to mention, it certainly presents a more visually appealing spectacle than its counterpart on the left.

Now, observe this example of a template cover. While it might have enjoyed popularity in the past, its excessive use by self-publishers has rendered it almost synonymous with amateurish work. It's in your best interest to avoid such commonplace designs to ensure your book stands out from the masses.

Below, you will find a variety of book covers all employing the same template and listed under the keyword "Puppy training for beginners." However, a few manage to distinguish themselves from the rest. Are you able to identify the ones that stand out?

Flip to the next page to discover the answer and see if your picks match up!

Did you select the covers numbered three and six? Great job! These two indeed stand out from the crowd, showcasing their individual flair. From an objective standpoint, they have a superior performance compared to the others, and their impressive BSR on Amazon is a solid testament to their strong sales performance!

Best-Selling Book Covers

Here are some covers from best-selling books. Take a look at them to get ideas and inspiration as you work on creating your own masterpiece.

Notice how seamlessly the cover image complements the book's topic? It feels natural and enhances the overall book.

Final Thoughts

Contrary to popular sayings, it's true that people do judge a book by its cover. After pouring your passion and effort into creating your book, the last thing you should skimp on is the cover. To stand out in the vast Amazon marketplace, your book deserves a professionally crafted, eye-catching cover. A visually appealing cover can make a significant difference in attracting readers. As you continue your journey in the world of publishing, you'll develop a knack for identifying great covers, grasping their appeal, and working with a designer to create a cover that perfectly suits your niche.

14

UPLOADING YOUR EBOOK

Uploading your book to Amazon is a breeze in your self-publishing journey, whether it's a Kindle eBook or a paperback. It's a step simpler than writing the book itself, formatting it, or diving into the world of promotion. After you've successfully set up your KDP account, you'll find that the process of uploading your book will only require a few minutes of your time.

To begin, simply log in to your KDP account. As you sign in, you'll be directed to your personalized KDP page. This hub offers various tabs for easy navigation, including Bookshelf, Reports, Community, and Marketing. By default, you'll land on your Bookshelf, where you can effortlessly upload new books.

On the KDP page, prominently displayed in large type, you'll notice the inviting phrase "Create. Manage. Publish." Right below this, you'll encounter a field labeled "Create a new title or series." Amazon kindly informs you that it's possible to reach readers in various formats such as eBooks, paperbacks, and hardcovers. In case you're working on a series, Amazon makes it convenient for you to create an Amazon series page and seamlessly add your books to it.

Now, let's narrow our focus to the process of uploading a Kindle eBook. To initiate this process, you'll want to click on the yellow "+ Create" button. This will promptly transport you to a fresh page titled "What would you like to create?" Inside the Kindle eBook square, there's another inviting yellow button that beckons you: "Create eBook." Give it a click, and you'll find yourself navigating through a series of three pages.

Our journey begins with the first page, bearing the title "Kindle eBook Details." This page boasts several sections that call for your attention and input.

Language

The initial field that demands your attention is the "Language" section. This field is intelligently configured to match the language of the Amazon site where you're registered. For instance, if you're embarking on your publishing journey in the United States, you'll find that the default language is English. Nevertheless, Amazon graciously extends the option to publish your literary creations in a diverse array of languages. This includes, but is not limited to, Afrikaans, Arabic, Danish, Dutch, Finnish, French, German, Italian, Japanese, Portuguese, Spanish, Swedish, and many more.

As you advance through your self-publishing odyssey, it's worth contemplating the prospect of translating and presenting your literary works in multiple languages. This strategic move has the potential to yield significant benefits by expanding your reach to a wider and more diverse audience. Drawing from my personal experience, I made the decision to translate my best-selling book into Spanish, German, and French. The results were remarkable: while the Spanish and German versions consistently garnered a steady stream of monthly sales, the French iteration exceeded all expectations, securing its position as my fourth best-selling book this year.

However, a piece of prudent advice would be to contemplate this step when you've established a strong foundation with a portfolio of at least ten published books and a steady monthly income of at least $1,000. Venturing into translations can be a costly endeavor, and entering new markets inherently carries some level of risk. Therefore, it's advisable to be well-prepared before taking this significant step.

It's essential to note that while Chat is a remarkable tool, it currently lacks the capability to perform precise book translations. Language nuances can be quite intricate, and Chat may not accurately capture these subtleties, potentially leading to inaccuracies in translations. Attempting to translate and publish books using Chat may result in less-than-ideal reviews from readers who encounter a subpar and error-ridden reading experience.

Book Title

When you proceed to the next section, you'll be prompted to enter the title of your book. Here, you should provide the primary title of your book as well as your subtitle. It's important to keep in mind that you have the flexibility to modify your Kindle book titles even after they've been published. However, this flexibility doesn't extend to paperback books. Additionally, it's crucial to ensure that the title and subtitle for your paperback version perfectly match your cover design, as Amazon mandates this alignment for publication.

Your Kindle and paperback book titles don't necessarily have to be identical, however, to simplify the process, create a single title that incorporates the main keywords for both the Kindle and paperback versions. Place this combined title in the main title box, using a '-' to separate the main title from the subtitle. For instance, you can format it as: "The Ketogenic Cook Book - A Beginner's Guide To Learning The Keto Diet."

Book Title	Enter your title as it appears on the book cover. This field cannot be changed after your book is published. Learn more about book titles.
	Book Title
	The Ketogenic Cook Book - A Beginner' Guide To Learning The Keto Diet
	Subtitle (Optional)

Series

If your book is part of a series, you have the option to provide series details to help readers discover your other works easily on a single detail page. You can either include the title you're currently uploading in an existing series or start a new series. Once you've completed this setup, any linked formats for the title will automatically become part of the series. This allows readers to view all available formats for your series titles on a single page and select the one that suits their preferences.

Creating a series also allows you to establish a reading order for your audience. You can assign numbers to the titles for a sequential reading experience or leave them unordered, allowing readers to enjoy them in any order they prefer. If you have different language versions of your series titles, it's advisable to create separate series for each language. This ensures that readers can easily find all the titles in your series in their preferred language.

In the early stages of your publishing journey, you may not have a series to consider, so don't worry too much about this aspect for now.

Edition Number

In the "Edition Number" field, you have the option to specify the edition of your book. If your book is the first edition or a new edition of an existing book, you can enter the appropriate edition number. For example, if you initially published your book and later made significant revisions or updates to create a new version, you can indicate it as the second edition. It's worth mentioning that providing an edition number is not mandatory.

From my personal experience, I would suggest publishing a new version instead of revising and updating an old one. This way, you'll have two separate listings, potentially doubling your earnings. This approach can be particularly advantageous for books with titles like "The 2023 Cookbook" and "The 2024 Cookbook" (please note that creating a cookbook is not recommended and is just used as an example).

Author

When filling out the "Author" field, make sure to provide the first and last name of the main author or contributor of the book. This can be your legal name or a pen name that you've selected. Keep in mind that once your book is published on Kindle or paperback, it's not possible to change the author's name.

Contributors

If there are other individuals who have contributed to your book, such as co-authors, editors, illustrators, or translators, you have the option to include their names in the contributors section. You can also indicate their specific roles, such as author, editor, illustrator, introduction writer, narrator, photographer, preface writer, or translator. However, if you are the primary author of the book, you only need to list your name in the author section and do not need to duplicate it under contributors.

Description

The description section serves a vital role in attracting potential customers and influencing their decision to purchase your book. You have the option to utilize HTML code or Amazon's formatting features to enhance the description, allowing for the inclusion of elements like bold text, italics, underlining, numbers, bullets, and paragraphs.

When crafting your book description, Amazon recommends maintaining simplicity, compelling content, and a professional tone. Your goal should be to convey the main plot, theme, or idea of your book in a clear and engaging manner, avoiding any potential confusion for readers. It's advisable to use concise sentences that are easy to read, particularly within a 150-word paragraph.

To capture the reader's attention, consider starting with a memorable opening sentence, and be sure to clearly indicate the genre of your book. Seeking feedback from others can be helpful in refining the description.

While Amazon imposes certain restrictions on the content of descriptions, such as prohibiting offensive material, personal contact information, reviews or testimonials, time-sensitive information, and promotional material, successful self-published authors have a trick up their sleeves. By strategically incorporating relevant keywords into your description, you can increase the discoverability of your book. The key is to integrate these keywords into engaging and informative sentences that make the description more appealing.

For example, if your book revolves around healthy eating and plant-based diets, you can craft an enticing sentence for your description like this: "Are you ready to embark on a journey to transform your health and embrace a vibrant lifestyle? Explore the world of nutritious plant-based eating and discover how to nourish your body with delicious and wholesome meals!" Keep in mind that the first four lines of your description are particularly important, as they are visible to customers before they click on "read more." Make sure these lines are attention-grabbing, and consider using bold formatting to make them stand out.

Publishing Rights

In the Publishing Rights section, you'll encounter two options. If you are the copyright holder and possess the necessary publishing rights for the content, choose the first option. This applies when you have authored the book yourself, and according to US copyright law, your work is automatically protected as soon as it's created. You have full ownership and can publish it without the need for a formal agreement with a publisher.

On the other hand, the second option, "This is a public domain work," should be selected when you are altering or translating a book that is already available for free on the Internet.

It's essential to note that until your book starts generating a substantial monthly income, typically in the multiple thousands of dollars range, there's no immediate need to pursue copyright registration. Copyright registration can be both costly and time-consuming, taking several months to complete. Regarding public domain works, this is not a viable strategy for building a lasting brand or generating significant income, so it's advisable to steer clear of this approach.

Keywords

When it comes to adding keywords to the backend of your books, there are a few factors to consider for optimal results. While the title and subtitle have character limits, Amazon offers an opportunity to include more keywords. There are two approaches you can take: either use a single keyword in each box or populate the boxes with multiple words.

An experiment conducted by someone in the publishing community tested these approaches to see which one was more effective. It turned out that having fewer words in each box gives more weight to those individual words compared to cramming multiple keywords into a single box. Therefore, it makes sense to go with the one-word-per-box strategy. If you've crafted a compelling title and subtitle, you may not need to add multiple keywords in each box. Additionally, remember to incorporate relevant keywords into your book description. If you have any remaining keywords, you can include them in the additional boxes provided (you have a total of seven).

To discover these keywords, pay attention to the suggestions that appear in Amazon's search field dropdown. Put yourself in the shoes of a reader and consider how they might search for a book. You can also analyze the keywords used in other popular books within your genre and incorporate relevant ones into your list.

Amazon does have some guidelines regarding keywords that are not recommended for use. These include keywords that already exist in your book's metadata (such as the title and contributors), subjective claims about the quality of your book (such as calling it the "best novel ever"), time-sensitive statements ("new," "on sale," "available now"), common information applicable to most books in the category (like "book"), spelling errors, and variations in spacing, punctuation, capitalization, and plurals. Additionally, avoid using Amazon program names like "Kindle Unlimited" or "KDP Select" as keywords.

In building a long-lasting business, it's advisable to err on the side of caution. By optimizing your title, description, and keywords, you can enhance the discoverability of your book on Amazon and increase the likelihood of reaching your target readers.

Categories

Selecting the right categories for your book is a crucial step. When setting up your Kindle eBook and paperback versions, you have the option to choose three categories for each format. However, there's an interesting twist: the categories available for Kindle eBooks and paperbacks are not the same. Surprisingly, this can work to your advantage because it allows you to select different categories for each version right from the start. By doing so, you enhance your book's visibility across various platforms, attracting more attention and increasing your chances of making book sales.

Age & Grade Range

The "age and grade range" section is optional and primarily used for children's books. It enables parents to filter books by age suitability. If your books are intended for an adult audience, you can skip this section.

Pre-Orders

Pre-orders are commonly used by fiction authors to build anticipation among their fan base, especially for series where readers eagerly await the next installment. Some authors even set up pre-orders for multiple books in a series, particularly if they have a frequent release schedule. Amazon automatically notifies readers about upcoming books in a series, whether they are on pre-order or already available. However, it's important to note that pre-orders are not available for paperback books. If you're publishing both a Kindle and paperback version, consider uploading the paperback a few days ahead of the scheduled Kindle release, as Amazon's approval process for paperbacks may take longer.

Non-fiction books typically do not use pre-orders. While it's an option, many non-fiction authors find that it doesn't significantly impact sales, so it's not a common practice in this genre. This can be a relief for non-fiction authors, as it simplifies the publishing process.

Second Page

Once you've finished filling out the first page on KDP, you have the option to either save your progress as a draft or save and continue. Choosing the latter will lead you to the second page, where you can proceed with uploading your manuscript. It's important to keep in mind that while many details can be modified before finalizing your book's publication, certain fields, are not editable once saved. Therefore, it's essential to thoroughly review and confirm the accuracy of the information you've provided before moving on to the next stage of the publishing process.

Digital Rights Management

Amazon provides authors with the option to enable DRM (Digital Rights Management) for their Kindle books. DRM is designed to prevent unauthorized distribution of your book file. However, some authors decide not to apply DRM because they may want to encourage readers to share their work.

If you choose to enable DRM, readers will still be able to lend the book to another user for a limited time or purchase it as a gift from the Kindle store. It's important to note that once your book is published, you cannot change its DRM setting.

Personally, I prefer to leave the DRM option unchecked, as it's the default setting. Amazon likely has valid reasons for this choice. It's essential to understand that determined individuals who want to obtain your book illegally may find ways to do so, even with DRM measures in place. Therefore, trying to prevent such actions may not always be effective.

Upload Book Manuscript

Uploading your book manuscript is the next step in the process. Depending on how you created your file, whether it's in Word (.DOCX), made using Kindle Create, Vellum, or with assistance from someone else, you can click on the yellow button and select the file from your computer. You can upload a new version of your book anytime you need to make updates.

If Amazon detects a potential spelling error in your manuscript file, you'll see an alert. You can click on the potential error to check if it's a legitimate mistake or if it's an unrecognized slang or term. If it's indeed an error, you can make the necessary corrections in your Word document, reformat the file using Kindle Create, and then upload the updated version. If the word is not a spelling error, you can simply click the "ignore" button.

Kindle eBook Cover

Moving forward, you'll need to upload your book's cover in the next field. Amazon provides two options for this section: you can use the Cover Creator tool, which lets you design a cover using Amazon's templates (though it's not recommended), or you can upload a cover you already have in JPG or TIFF format. Ensure that all the necessary files are uploaded before proceeding to the third and final page of the listing form.

Once your manuscript and cover files have been processed, you'll need to click on the "launch previewer" option to review and approve the files. It's important to note that Amazon may take some time to process these files, sometimes up to ten or twenty minutes. So, if you encounter a delay, don't worry; it's perfectly normal.

ISBN

ISBN, which stands for International Standard Book Number, serves as an identifier for books. While Kindle eBooks do not require an ISBN, it is mandatory for paperback books. The decision to acquire ISBNs becomes especially significant if you plan to self-publish your books on platforms other than Amazon. So for now, just use the free ISBN Amazon gives you.

From a practical standpoint, if I were starting anew, I wouldn't spend too much time contemplating the purchase of ISBNs and going wide. The majority of your book sales are likely to come from Amazon, so it's more effective to focus your efforts there, following the 80/20 rule. The additional effort, time, and expenses associated with uploading your book to other platforms and acquiring ISBNs may not be justified. You can use the free ISBN provided by Amazon, publish your book, and then move on to creating your next one.

Third Page

On the third and final page, you'll encounter some essential steps in the publishing process. This is where you'll set your eBook's pricing and distribution options. Let's dive into these steps in more detail.

KDP Select Enrollment

Now, let's discuss the KDP Select enrollment, which is located at the top of the third and final page. We discussed this earlier but here's a quick recap of what it entails. KDP Select is Amazon's Kindle Unlimited program, allowing Amazon customers to pay a monthly subscription fee for access to and borrowing of eligible Kindle books.

To make your book available for Kindle Unlimited subscribers to read for free, you need to voluntarily enroll it in the KDP Select program. This program primarily consists of self-published works, as traditionally published books are rarely enrolled in KDP Select. Under this program, Amazon collects Kindle Unlimited subscription fees and distributes the revenue among authors whose books were downloaded by Kindle Unlimited subscribers.

Currently, the payout for KDP Select is approximately half a cent per page read. This means that authors earn around one penny for every two pages read by subscribers. It's important to note that Amazon tracks page-reads based on physical page turns by the reader, so authors are no longer paid for skipped pages.

Enrolling your Kindle books in KDP Select provides several advantages, despite the requirement of exclusivity to Amazon for the eBook version during the enrollment period. Here are the key benefits:

- **Opportunity for Free Book Promotions:** With KDP Select, you can run promotions where your eBook is available for free for up to five days during each ninety-day enrollment period. This can significantly boost your book's visibility and potentially lead to more paperback sales or reviews from readers who obtained the eBook for free.

- **Kindle Countdown Deals:** KDP Select allows you to run Kindle Countdown Deals for books priced between $2.99 and $24.99. This feature enables you to offer your book at a discounted price for a limited time, creating a sense of urgency for potential buyers. It can be an effective marketing tool to drive sales.

Enrolling your Kindle book in KDP Select does come with a requirement of exclusivity to Amazon for a ninety-day period, but it's a strategic choice for many authors. During this time, the exclusivity applies only to the eBook version of your book, allowing you the freedom to publish the paperback version on alternative platforms.

In my perspective, it's a smart move to have your book enrolled in the KDP Select program, especially for the initial ninety days. Amazon tends to prioritize and promote books within its own program, which can significantly boost your book's visibility and potential for success. While success isn't impossible without enrolling, opting for this exclusivity period can enhance your book's chances of gaining traction and achieving your goals.

Territories

In the Territories section, Amazon offers you the choice to make your book available either worldwide or in specific individual territories. To reach the widest audience, you can simply select "All territories (worldwide rights)." This option enables customers from various Amazon websites around the world, including but not limited to the US, UK, Germany, France, Spain, Italy, Japan, Netherlands, Brazil, Mexico, Canada, India, Australia, and more, to purchase your book. It's a great way to expand your book's reach to a global audience.

Primary Marketplace

In the Primary Marketplace section, you can choose the main Amazon website where you expect most of your book sales to occur. If it's not already set to Amazon.com for the United States, I highly recommend making that adjustment. Based on my experience, and likely for you as well, around 95% of your sales will originate from this marketplace.

Pricing, Royalty & Distribution

As an author, you have the freedom to set the price of your books on Amazon, and they offer different royalty options based on the price and delivery method.

For books priced between 99 cents and $2.98, or those priced at $10 or more, you can opt for a 35% payout. This option doesn't incur a delivery fee, making it suitable for lower-priced or large file size books. To maximize sales, I recommend setting your book at 99 cents for the first month.

On the other hand, books priced between $2.99 and $9.99, which is the majority range for Kindle eBooks, can earn a 70% payout. This option does have a delivery fee of 15 cents per megabyte. Once the initial thirty days have passed, I suggest increasing the eBook price to $2.99.

Consider that pricing strategies can be influenced by various factors, such as your book's genre, its length, and the perceived value it offers to readers. When you distribute your book globally through Amazon, they automatically adjust the price to match local currencies.

In terms of KDP Select enrollment and pricing, my approach has evolved over time. Initially, I set my Kindle book prices at $2.99 and enrolled them in KDP Select. However, as I began writing longer non-fiction works, I increased the price to $9.99 and withdrew them from KDP Select. It's noteworthy that with outright purchases on Amazon, authors receive payment regardless of whether readers actually read the book. Even years later, I continue to earn royalties from pages read by readers who initially downloaded my books through KDP Select.

For your debut book, launching it at a price of 99 cents with a 30% royalty rate can be advantageous. This lower price point may stimulate sales and facilitate the gathering of valuable reviews, which play a pivotal role in enhancing your book's visibility and future sales. It's essential to remember that you can always adjust the price as your book gains momentum. If you lack a substantial following on social media, enrolling your initial book in KDP Select and making it available for borrowing by Kindle Unlimited members can be a sound strategy. While the earnings per page read may seem modest, these borrows can potentially lead to reviews and contribute to an improved ranking for your book. As a new author, your initial readers may opt to borrow rather than purchase your book, making their reviews all the more important for future sales.

To encourage readers to leave reviews, consider including a friendly note at the conclusion of your book, kindly requesting their feedback and providing a QR code (easily generated for free on Canva.com) that directs them straight to the review page. Although Amazon prompts readers to leave reviews and guides them to the book's detail page, a personal request can be particularly effective.

Speaking of which, would you mind taking thirty seconds to leave a quick review? Maybe if you do, the karma will come back around and people reading your future books will leave one too! Scan the QR code and that will take you straight to the Amazon review page!

It's not uncommon for novice authors to hesitate when pricing their books lower, often feeling that their work merits higher pricing. However, it's important acknowledge the highly competitive landscape of the Kindle market, where numerous self-published authors vie for the attention of readers. Many of these authors have been publishing for several years. As someone with experience in Kindle eBook authorship since 2019, I've come to realize that it takes time and the cultivation of a dedicated readership before justifying the pricing of Kindle eBooks at $9.99.

Book Lending

Book lending is a feature that enables users to lend digital books they've purchased from the Kindle Store to friends and family. Each book can be lent once, for a duration of fourteen days, during which the lender temporarily loses access to the book. It's important to clarify that book lending is exclusively available for Kindle books bought on Amazon.

If you've acquired a copy of your own book, you do have the ability to lend it. However, the Kindle Book Lending program restricts loans to one per title, and such loans do not result in royalty payments.

By default, all titles under KDP are automatically enrolled in lending. Nevertheless, for titles utilizing the 35% royalty option, you have the option to opt-out of lending during the title setup process by unchecking the box in the "Book Lending" section. It's essential to note that opting out is not possible for titles using the 70% royalty option or titles included in the lending program of another sales or distribution channel.

Drawing from my own experience, I no longer enable book lending for my books. Although I initially allowed it, I found that book lending has become less popular over time. Consequently, my preference now leans towards having readers either borrow my books through KDP Select or purchase them outright, enabling me to generate income.

Publishing Your eBook

When you're ready to publish your Kindle eBook, ensure that all the required sections are correctly filled out. Once everything is in order, you'll see the orange "Publish Your Kindle eBook" button at the bottom of the page. It's important to note that it might take up to seventy-two hours for Amazon to make your Kindle eBook available on their website. The positive aspect is that you can make modifications to most of the fields even after your eBook has been published.

15

UPLOADING YOUR PAPERBACK

Creating Your Paperback

To create a paperback edition of your book, the process closely resembles that of uploading the Kindle version. After your Kindle eBook is published, you'll find it on your KDP account's Bookshelf. Click on the "+ Create paperback" link to initiate the process.

Transitioning your Kindle eBook to a paperback is made easier, with some fields auto-filled. Yet, you can still edit most of them. One unique field is the Adult Content section, where you declare if your book contains material unsuitable for under-eighteens. Choose between NO or YES, but typically, unless it's a children's book, NO is the way to go.

Once you hit "Save & Continue" on the first page, you'll proceed to the second page where you'll furnish more paperback book details. Printed books need an ISBN, and you have two options: buy ISBNs from Bowker.com or utilize Amazon's free KDP ISBN (for now, the latter is a good choice).

When it comes to the Publication Date field, there's a simple guideline to follow: if your book has previously been published on another platform, enter the date of its initial publication (just a heads-up so you know why it's there). However, if this marks your book's first-ever publication, feel free to bypass this section. Amazon will automatically populate the date once your book becomes available on their website. Additionally, note that the pre-order option is exclusive to Kindle books and cannot be applied to paperback versions.

Paperback Options

Paperback books come with a variety of options for their page interiors, and Amazon provides the following choices for Ink and Paper Types:

- Black and white interior with cream paper: Typically used for fiction and memoirs, this option offers a paper weight of 55 pounds.
- Black and white interior with white paper: Amazon's default selection, commonly used for nonfiction books, also with a paper weight of 55 pounds.
- Standard color interior with white paper: This is a more affordable option for books that contain color, although it's not recommended for those with full-color page elements. It offers a paper weight of 55 pounds.
- Premium color interior with white paper: This option is suitable for books with full-color elements such as illustrations, graphics, and images, offering a paper weight of 60 pounds.

Trim Size: The trim size is all about the dimensions of the pages within your paperback book. Amazon offers a range of sizes, with 5x8 (12.7x20.32 cm) inches or 6x9 (15.24x22.86 cm) inches being the most commonly chosen dimensions for self-published non-fiction books.

Bleed Settings: Bleed settings are related to printing, specifically printing at or off the edge of a page to support images and illustrations. In most cases, "no bleed" is the standard choice, unless there's a specific requirement for bleed.

Paperback Cover Finish: When it comes to the finish of your paperback book cover, Amazon provides two options: glossy and matte. The glossy finish gives a shiny appearance, enhancing black covers and artwork, while the matte cover finish offers a subtle, polished look with minimal sheen. The choice between the two is a matter of personal preference. For example, I personally prefer matte covers for all my books as they provide a premium feel when held.

Manuscript: In this section, you'll need to upload the file for your paperback book. Amazon supports various file formats, including PDF, DOC, DOCX, HTML, and RTF.

Book Cover: Here, you'll upload your own print-ready PDF file for the paperback book cover. It's important to note that the paperback book cover is different from the Kindle version, as it includes a spine and back cover in addition to the front cover.

Launch Preview: After uploading your manuscript and cover, you can click the "Launch Previewer" button. Amazon will process these uploads, which may take some time. Before moving on to the final page, preview and accept the complete file of your book.

Summary: On the second page of the book listing, you'll find the Summary section. This section displays the complete file of your book, including the cover and interior pages as they will appear in print. Amazon will also show you the printing cost, which will be automatically deducted from the sale price of your book. Once you've reviewed and approved the file, you can proceed to the third and final page.

Third Page

Third Page: When you reach the third page of the publishing process, you'll encounter the Territories section, which is similar to what you experienced when uploading the Kindle version of your book. Here, you'll decide whether to make your paperback book available worldwide (with worldwide rights) or select specific regions. It's generally advisable to select worldwide rights to maximize your book's reach.

The Primary Marketplace field on this page determines the primary marketplace where your book will be available. By default, it will be set to the country you are uploading from. For example, if you're uploading from the United States, the default will be Amazon.com. Regardless of your location, it's recommended to set your default marketplace to Amazon.com, as this is where the majority of sales typically come from.

Pricing, Royalty, & Distribution

For paperback books, publishers earn a 60% royalty. This royalty is calculated after deducting Amazon's share of the purchase price and the printing cost, which can vary based on factors such as the number of pages and trim size of your book.

It's worth mentioning that while international buyers will see the price you set for your book, it's important to understand that paperback books are not as widely distributed as Kindle eBooks.

Publish Your Paperback Book

Once you've set the price for your paperback book, simply click the "Publish your paperback book" button to make it available on Amazon's website. Unlike Kindle eBooks, which are usually approved within a day, paperback books may take several days for approval. This is because Amazon meticulously reviews each paperback to ensure it will print correctly when ordered, guaranteeing a high-quality reading experience for customers.

Request Proof Copies

After successfully publishing your paperback book, you have the option to request proof copies at a discounted rate. This enables you to physically review the book and make any necessary adjustments before offering it for purchase. Alternatively, you can order copies directly from the Amazon website. This not only benefits your author rank but also allows you to earn royalties from the sales of those copies.

<u>Hardcovers</u>

The procedure for uploading and publishing the hardcover version of your book is the same as what you've just followed for the paperback. Simply repeat the steps to get your hardback edition published.

16

AUDIOBOOKS

Audiobooks have become a significant game-changer in the ever-evolving publishing industry. They offer a flexible and engaging format that resonates with today's fast-paced society. Uploading your content to platforms like Audible opens up exciting opportunities and broadens your potential audience. Audiobooks not only cater to those with reading difficulties or visual impairments but also attract individuals who prefer auditory learning or want to consume content while on the go, whether commuting, exercising, or doing daily tasks. Additionally, the increasing use of digital technology and smartphones has made accessing audiobooks more convenient than ever. Venturing into the world of audiobooks unlocks numerous advantages, expanding your reach and influence as an author.

Where Should I Begin with Audiobook Creation?

If you're considering entering the audiobook market, Audible is the primary platform to target for your audiobook debut. Following the 80/20 rule, concentrating on Audible can efficiently reach the majority of your audiobook audience. However, to get started, authors need to go to acx.com instead of audible.com. By creating an account on ACX, you can claim your books from Amazon and initiate your audiobook creation journey.

Acx.com also serves as an excellent marketplace for finding the perfect narrator for your audiobook project. Narrator rates can vary widely, ranging from $40 to several hundred dollars per finished hour. But what does "per finished hour" mean? Essentially, it refers to the cost of one hour of polished, fully narrated audio. While the actual narration, recording, and audio cleanup may take longer than an hour, the fee is determined based on the finished hour, providing a transparent pricing structure.

For our audiobook targets, aiming for books around 30,000 words is ideal. This is because approximately every 10,000 words result in one hour of narration. Therefore, a 30,000-word book would typically yield about three hours of audiobook content, which is the sweet spot we aim for. Audible offers an approximate $7 royalty for a three-hour audiobook. If the audiobook falls just shy of the three-hour mark at two hours and fifty-nine minutes, the royalty drops to approximately $3. However, audiobooks spanning five to ten hours in length will earn around $10 in royalties. In simpler terms, the 3-5 hour range tends to offer the highest payment for the fewest words. It's important to note that Audible sets the prices based on the audiobook's length, and authors do not have control over the pricing. Below, you'll find more details on the royalty structure:

Audiobook Length	Retail Price	Net Sales $
< 1hr	3.95	2.05
1-3 hrs	6.95	3.61
3-5 hrs	14.95	7.77
5-10 hrs	19.95	10.37
10-20 hrs	24.95	12.97
20 hrs +	29.95	15.57

If your 30,000-word audiobook falls short of the three-hour mark, it's likely because the narrator read too quickly. Generally, it takes approximately 27,000 words spoken at a normal pace to reach the three-hour duration. Therefore, a 30,000-word audiobook should be more than enough to meet this mark. To avoid any last-minute surprises, it's essential to communicate your desired audiobook length with the narrator beforehand. This ensures that the final product aligns with your expectations.

My Reflections

Starting your author journey with audiobooks might not be the best strategy when you're just getting started. It's advisable to focus on creating a few high-quality books initially. By doing so, you can become familiar with the publishing process, grasp the intricacies of writing, and accumulate valuable writing experience before venturing into audiobooks. It's a step-by-step approach that allows you to build a solid foundation.

Once your books begin generating a consistent monthly income of at least $500, that's when you should consider exploring the world of audiobooks. This approach has the added financial benefit of using the income from your books to cover the costs associated with producing an audiobook. Typically, for a 30,000-word book, the narration cost will be around $150.

In essence, it's a gradual progression that ensures you're well-prepared and financially supported when you decide to dive into the realm of audiobooks.

17

PRICING YOUR BOOKS

Setting the price for your books is not solely about maximizing your income but also about enticing potential readers to make a purchase. It's about finding that delicate equilibrium between a reasonable price and broad customer appeal.

Pricing Low-Content Books

When it comes to low-content books like journals, planners, coloring books, and activity books, they are typically priced in the range of $3.99 to $9.99. The optimal price point often hovers around $6.99, which provides a $2 profit per book. It can be challenging to sell these types of books at a higher price due to stiff competition from similar quality books at lower prices. This is one of the reasons why some authors choose to avoid low-content books.

Pricing Fiction Books

For fiction authors, understanding the pricing dynamics in this genre is essential. Whether you're following the traditional publishing path or self-publishing on Amazon, fiction books typically have lower price points, and these prices often decrease over time. Even a best-selling author's hardcover might debut at $19.99 but could quickly drop to $9.99 or even $6.99 for the paperback edition. EBooks, in particular, can be priced as low as one or two dollars.

For self-published authors, it's not realistic to initially price your first fiction book at $20 or even $10. Instead, your focus should be on building an audience and possibly enrolling in Kindle Select to earn a share of Kindle Unlimited membership fees. In the early stages, your goal is to gain visibility, improve your rankings, and accumulate positive reviews. Significant profits are more likely to come later in your publishing journey.

The pricing of fiction books, typically on the lower side, can be attributed to several factors. Firstly, the fiction genre enjoys a broad readership, and self-published authors frequently release new books, often with shorter word counts. Unlike traditionally published novels, which often exceed 80,000 words, self-published books can be as short as 30,000 words or even less. This abundance of shorter works caters to avid readers who consume multiple books each week, providing them with a wider selection to choose from at lower price points.

Pricing Non-Fiction Books

Determining the appropriate pricing strategy for non-fiction books involves a different approach. Non-fiction works typically offer valuable information, expertise, or unique perspectives to readers. Therefore, pricing should align with the book's value and the perceived benefit it offers. Non-fiction books generally have higher price points compared to fiction. The actual price range can vary depending on factors like the subject matter, depth of research, and the author's credentials. Readers are often willing to invest more in books that provide specialized knowledge, well-researched content, and practical guidance.

When setting the price for your non-fiction book, it's crucial to take into account your target audience, competitive landscape, and the unique aspects of your work. Conduct thorough market research, analyze similar titles, and assess what readers are willing to pay for the specific subject matter you cover.

In my own practice, I typically price my non-fiction books within the range of $12.99 to $29.99, taking into consideration the competition and their pricing strategies. If you have a substantial number of reviews compared to your competitors, you may be able to justify a higher price point. However, if there is significant competition with lower prices, it's advisable to stay within that competitive range. An effective method for testing pricing is to start with a lower price and gradually increase it by a dollar every two weeks while monitoring sales. If sales remain steady, you can continue to incrementally raise the price until you notice a decline in sales. This approach allows you to find the optimal price point for your non-fiction book.

Hardcovers

When it comes to pricing hardcover editions of books, my usual approach is to set the price approximately $10 higher than that of the paperback edition. This strategy is grounded in three key reasons.

Firstly, hardcovers generally incur higher production costs. To ensure authors receive a comparable royalty from hardcovers, pricing them at a premium is necessary.

Secondly, this pricing strategy leverages a psychological technique known as price anchoring. Imagine going to a restaurant and seeing a menu where high-end steaks are listed at $100. Then, you come across a burger priced at $40. Initially, the $40 burger seems like a more affordable choice when contrasted with the $100 steaks. This is due to the higher-priced steaks acting as an anchor, causing the burger to appear as a better value by comparison (even though a $40 burger would be exorbitantly priced in any other setting!). By implementing price anchoring, the restaurant strategically influences customers to view the $40 burger as a better deal, increasing the likelihood of them selecting it over other options.

Setting a higher price for hardcovers creates a price anchor that shapes readers' perception of the paperback's price. Consequently, the paperback edition seems relatively more affordable and offers superior value.

The third rationale behind this approach is that some readers have a preference for hardcovers and are willing to pay the higher price. By pricing hardcovers at, for example, $24.99 or $29.99, authors can earn a substantial royalty of $10 or more per book sold.

In summary, pricing hardcovers at a premium compared to paperbacks serves multiple purposes: it accounts for production costs, employs price anchoring to enhance the perceived value of the paperback, and attracts readers who favor hardcovers, ultimately increasing royalty earnings.

18

MARKETING & SOCIAL MEDIA

During my journey as an author, I've explored various marketing strategies. Given my prior experience with Instagram, I initially focused on this platform. I managed to grow an Instagram account to over 200,000 followers for one of my brands. However, I soon realized that the return on investment (ROI) wasn't as favorable as I had hoped. The considerable time and effort required for daily posting and content creation didn't align with the sales generated. It became clear that my time could be better spent creating more books rather than managing Instagram.

I also ventured into Facebook advertising, but this avenue proved to be expensive and resulted in relatively low conversion rates. The multi-step process of capturing users' attention, encouraging them to read the ad, click on it, visit the product page on Amazon, add the book to their cart, and ultimately make a purchase presented significant challenges.

Drawing from my personal experiences, I found that social media marketing didn't deliver substantial results. While some individuals may excel in this domain or opt to enlist marketing agencies, it demands a significant investment of time, finances, and mental energy. In my view, it's not the most efficient approach.

Keeping in line with the 80/20 rule, it's crucial to concentrate on strategies that genuinely drive revenue. Does establishing an Instagram account directly contribute to your income? Do Facebook groups or accumulating likes equate to profits? Does reposting tweets or pinning on Pinterest translate into financial gains? The answer, in most cases, is no.

However, there's one method I've discovered that proves to be a valuable time investment, particularly if you intend to create multiple books under the same pen name or brand: email collection. You can incorporate a QR code throughout your book inviting readers to subscribe for additional bonus content. By building an email list, you establish a direct line of communication with these readers when you release another book. This audience is more inclined to make a repeat purchase since they've already bought from you once. Furthermore, you can politely request book reviews via email, bolstering your book's visibility.

The setup of an email collection system is a one-time effort that operates in the background. Once your book is available on Amazon and generating sales, you'll automatically begin gathering emails from interested readers.

I personally utilize an email software called Convertkit. At the time of composing this, you can sign up for free and collect up to 1,000 emails before you need to consider a paid plan. They offer comprehensive tutorials on their platform to help you set up a simple email opt-in process (the process of collecting email addresses).

In return for the reader's email, you should provide them with a "freebie" or lead magnet. This is a valuable incentive or resource offered to potential subscribers or leads, serving as a way to attract and engage your target audience.

Lead magnets are meticulously crafted to tackle a specific problem or offer a solution that resonates with the interests and needs of your particular audience. Here are some examples of lead magnets tailored to various niches:

Health and Fitness

• Meal plan or recipe eBook: Extend a complimentary eBook featuring healthy recipes or a guide to meal planning.

• Workout video or fitness guide: Grant access to a video workout session or a comprehensive fitness guide.

Personal Development

• Goal-setting worksheet: Share a downloadable worksheet designed to assist individuals in defining and accomplishing their goals.

• Productivity toolkit: Provide a toolkit loaded with productivity resources like templates, checklists, and guides.

Finance

• Budgeting template: Offer a spreadsheet template or recommend a helpful app for effective financial management.

• Investment guide: Deliver an eBook or a series of videos delving into investment strategies and tips.

Marketing and Business

• Social media content calendar: Supply a pre-made content calendar to aid businesses in planning their social media posts.

• Marketing toolkit: Assemble a collection of marketing templates, guides, and resources.

Travel

• Destination guide: Furnish a downloadable guide packed with insider insights, tips, and recommendations for a popular travel destination.

• Packing checklist: Provide a checklist detailing essential items to pack for various types of trips.

Remember, the crux of a successful lead magnet is its ability to offer value, relevance, and alignment with the interests of your target audience. It should present a swift win or resolution to a challenge they're encountering, while also showcasing your expertise and cultivating trust.

19

AMAZON ADS FOR AUTHORS

In the realm of book sales, directing your marketing efforts towards customers already present on Amazon, primed for a purchase, streamlines the entire process. This is precisely why I've made the deliberate choice to exclusively advertise my books on Amazon, utilizing their native advertising platform.

While the notion of investing in ads on a platform where your books are readily available might initially seem counterintuitive, the reality is that you're contending with a vast sea of competing titles. Unless you're the fortunate holder of an instant best-seller, harnessing the power of Amazon Advertising becomes indispensable for securing visibility and propelling sales for your paperback editions.

Amazon's own data underscores this necessity, revealing that a significant 30% of readers frequently engage with Amazon explicitly in search of books. Additionally, an impressive 65% of readers stumble upon fresh literary discoveries while actively perusing the platform for their shopping needs. This data paints a vivid picture of an audience that is not only receptive but also actively on the lookout for new reading material. Advertising, in this context, presents an invaluable opportunity to connect with customers as they explore a wide array of book categories, positioning your work front and center for their consideration.

Different Advertising Methods

Various advertising methods are at your disposal when promoting your books on Amazon, and the platform offers three distinct options, each with its unique advantages.

The first option is Sponsored Products, which are cost-per-click (CPC) ads designed to promote individual product listings on Amazon. These ads enjoy prominent placement on the first page of search results and product pages. You retain control over your desired CPC bid, and you only pay when a customer clicks on your ad. Setting a daily budget enables you to effectively manage your expenses.

The second choice is Sponsored Brands, another CPC ad format that showcases not just your book but your brand logo, a concise headline, and multiple products. These ads are strategically positioned at the top and bottom of search results, making them particularly beneficial if you have a series or several related books. Similar to Sponsored Product Ads, you only incur charges when a customer clicks on your ad, and you retain control over both the per-click price and daily budget.

Lastly, Lockscreen Ads are a unique option available to US-based publishers. These ads make an appearance on Amazon devices like Kindle e-readers and Fire tablets, displaying your book prominently on the screen before users access their devices. However, it's important to acknowledge that Lockscreen Ads can be relatively pricier and are typically favored by authors with a well-established and substantial following.

For most self-published authors, the primary focus lies on Sponsored Product Ads and Sponsored Brand Ads due to their ease of management and learning curve. Personally, I have achieved success using Sponsored Product Ads, finding them to be a profitable avenue.

I suggest beginning your advertising journey with Sponsored Product Ads, and if you witness encouraging results, consider exploring the realm of Sponsored Brand Ads. However, I would strongly discourage the use of Lockscreen Ads. Speaking from personal experience as a Kindle owner, I seldom pay attention to the ads displayed on my screen, and I've even taken steps to disable them altogether. Given this, it's improbable that a user would come across an ad, click on it, and subsequently make a book purchase. Therefore, I find Lockscreen Ads to be less effective in driving book sales.

Getting Started with Ads

Embarking on your Amazon Advertising adventure begins with a simple and cost-free process: setting up an account at advertising.amazon.com. As you delve into advertising, you'll be required to connect a payment method, whether it's a credit card or direct bank withdrawals. Once your account is up and running, you're ready to dive into creating your very first ad campaign.

Within the Amazon Advertising dashboard, you'll spot a prominent blue "Create campaign" button eagerly waiting for your click, ushering you into the campaign creation realm. Here, you're presented with three options: Sponsored Products, Sponsored Brands, or Lockscreen Ads. As a starting point, opt for the default choice, Sponsored Products, and proceed by clicking the corresponding icon.

You'll first see Ad Format section, offering a choice between a Custom text ad or a Standard ad. With Custom text ads, you wield the power to infuse personalized text, providing potential customers with a sneak peek of your book. Meanwhile, Standard ads proudly showcase your book cover, star rating, and price. While both options suit non-fiction books admirably, Custom text ads can be a secret weapon for fiction books in the midst of fierce competition. For this example, let's embrace the allure of the Standard ad.

Progressing on your advertising adventure, you'll venture into the Products section, a pivotal point where you'll pinpoint the book that deserves the spotlight. While it might be tempting to promote both the Kindle and paperback editions, it's a savvy move to focus solely on advertising the paperback version. Here's why: Paperback ads allow customers to view the price upfront, making them more inclined to click and make a purchase at that visible price point. In contrast, advertising a $2.99 eBook could lead to campaigns that operate at a loss, with ad expenses surpassing the $2 profit gained from the sale.

Now, it's time to make a crucial decision: Automatic or Manual Targeting. If you're new to Amazon Advertising, the path of least resistance is Automatic Targeting. This option relies on Amazon's algorithm to identify keywords and products closely related to your ad content. In other words, Amazon plays matchmaker, connecting your book with potential readers who are likely to be interested. As you grow more comfortable with the process, Manual Targeting gives you the reins. You can handpick specific keywords or products to align with your ad. If you opt for Automatic Targeting, you'll encounter the default bid setting, which suggests starting with a conservative bid and adjusting it upward if needed. For those embracing Manual Targeting, you'll be presented with a choice between Keyword targeting and Product targeting.

With Keyword targeting, you're the architect of your campaign. You get to select particular keywords and short phrases that Amazon shoppers frequently type into the search bar. The power is in your hands: you can compile your keyword list, take advantage of Amazon's keyword suggestions, or combine both approaches. In contrast, Product targeting is like aiming a laser. You can pinpoint the exact products, categories, or brands you want to target with your ad. It's precision marketing at its finest.

In our example of setting up a Keyword Targeting ad for a Ketogenic cookbook, when you select your book, Amazon will automatically generate a list of relevant keywords based on what customers are actively searching for. Keep in mind that customers often use short phrases in their searches. Amazon's auto-fill suggestions offer valuable insights into popular keywords. These suggestions might include terms like "ketogenic diet recipes," "low-carb cooking," and "healthy fat recipes." Even if some of these keywords may appear unrelated to your book at first glance, they reflect active buying behavior and can be effective targets for your ad.

Back on the Amazon Advertising page, you'll have the option to either use Amazon's suggested keywords, input your own list, or upload a file containing your keyword list. For simplicity, let's focus on using the suggested keywords or entering your own list.

Before selecting keywords, determine your bidding price. Next to the "Bid" section, you'll see a bar displaying "Suggested bid." Clicking on it will reveal a drop-down menu with three choices: "Suggested bid," "Custom bid," and "Default bid." Initially, I made the mistake of relying on the suggested bids, which often exceeded the necessary amounts for effective ads and could quickly deplete your advertising budget. Instead, I recommend selecting "Custom bid," allowing you to set the same rate for each keyword. It's advisable to start with a very low bid. Amazon's suggested bids typically range from 50 cents to $1 or even higher. However, you can begin with a low custom bid of 30 cents, for example. Opting for an odd number like 21 cents can enhance competitiveness, as most advertisers prefer even numbers.

Once your bid rate is set, it's time to choose your keywords. Amazon categorizes keywords into three types: Broad, Phrase, and Exact.

Broad: With broad match keywords, your ads will appear for search terms that correspond to your keywords and related keywords, including synonyms, misspellings, and variations. For example, if you choose "Ketogenic Cookbook" as a broad match keyword, your ad might show up for searches like "Ketogeniccookbook" (misspelled), "Ketogenic Cookbooks," or "Keto cookbook."

Phrase: Phrase match keywords will display your ads for search terms that include the specific keywords in any order. For instance, if you select the keyword "Ketogenic Cookbook" as a phrase match, your ad could appear for searches like "Vegan Ketogenic Cookbook" or "Ketogenic Cookbook for beginners."

Exact: Exact match keywords will only trigger your ads when the search term precisely matches your chosen keywords. For example, if you set "Ketogenic Cookbook" as an exact match keyword, your ad will only be shown to users who search for "Ketogenic Cookbook" exactly.

When you're just starting out, it's perfectly fine to select all three keyword match types. Amazon typically pre-selects them by default. Over time, you'll learn which type works best for your campaign. I would begin with all three and slowly turn off the ones you see aren't working.

You can also let Amazon show your ads for all three types and manually choose your preferred options. Amazon will provide a comprehensive list of suggested keywords, but it's a good practice to review them. Manually selecting the relevant keywords and excluding the irrelevant ones is a wise approach.

Negative keyword targeting is an optional yet valuable feature. It allows you to exclude search terms that Amazon might use to target your ad but are irrelevant to your book. For instance, if you've authored a book on Personal Finance for teenagers, you wouldn't want your ad to appear for people searching for "personal finance for adults." By using negative keywords, you prevent Amazon from displaying your ad to users seeking a different book genre. It's a good practice to maintain a list of negative keywords for each of your books. When setting up a new ad campaign, you can manually enter these negative keywords by typing them or copying them from a file. Remember to add them as both Negative exact and Negative phrase to ensure they are effectively excluded.

Campaigns

In the Campaign section, you have the opportunity to select your Campaign bidding strategy. Amazon offers three options to consider:

• Dynamic bids - down only: With this strategy, Amazon will dynamically lower your bids in real-time when the likelihood of your ad converting to a sale decreases.

• Dynamic bids - up and down: Opting for this strategy allows Amazon to dynamically raise your bids by up to 100% when the chances of your ad leading to a sale increase, while also lowering bids when the likelihood decreases.

• Fixed bids: This strategy maintains your exact bid and any manual adjustments you've made, without changing your bids based on the likelihood of a sale.

For cost control, I personally prefer Dynamic bids - down only. Allowing Amazon to only lower your bid or stick to the bid price you set can help prevent excessive spending on ads.

Moving on to the Settings section, you'll begin by choosing a Campaign name. This can be the title of your book or a descriptive name to distinguish each ad if you plan to run multiple ads for the same book. Duplicate names for ads are not allowed in the system. As for my naming convention, I typically use a format like "Book name - manual/PA (product ad)/auto," for example:

1. Ketogenic (manual)

2. Ketogenic (PA)

3. Ketogenic (auto)

In the Start and End dates section, the default date will be set to the day you create the ad. It's generally advisable to leave the end date as "No end date." If you need to pause or stop the ad, you can do so directly from the main dashboard.

The Marketplace section is automatically selected based on your advertising country. For instance, if your account is in the United States, the United States marketplace will be pre-selected. Initially, it's recommended to focus on the US market, as it is the largest one. Once you have a book that gains significant traction and achieves substantial monthly earnings ($500+), you can then consider expanding your advertising efforts to other markets.

Next, determine your daily budget. Starting with a conservative budget of $5 is recommended. If your ad proves successful, you can increase your ad spending as needed later on.

After finalizing the settings, you have the option to save your ad as a draft or launch the campaign by clicking the blue "Launch campaign" button if you're ready for it to go live. You can edit or end your ads at any time, so there's no need to worry if you make a mistake along the way.

20

CONCLUSION

The realm of self-publishing presents a remarkable opportunity for aspiring authors. It offers the freedom to pursue one's publishing aspirations without the customary constraints associated with traditional publishing houses. In this domain, authors retain control over their creative journey and stand to reap a more substantial share of the rewards.

Nevertheless, it's imperative to recognize that self-publishing is a multifaceted endeavor that extends beyond the mere act of transferring thoughts onto paper. It entails critical responsibilities such as meticulous file formatting, the creation of compelling cover designs, and the execution of a well-structured promotional strategy. Success in self-publishing demands a dedicated investment of time and effort.

Fortunately, the insights and guidance provided within this book serve as a valuable resource to navigate the intricacies of self-publishing. Armed with this knowledge, you can approach the self-publishing world with confidence and competence, akin to a seasoned professional. Thus, seize the opportunities presented by self-publishing and embark on your authorial journey with assurance and purpose.

Reflecting on my personal journey, it becomes evident that, among my first ten books, only one achieved significant success, generating over $1,000 per month. It is essential to keep this valuable insight in mind as you embark on your own path. Your breakthrough might not occur immediately; it may require the creation of several books. However, this is entirely acceptable. The true measure of failure lies in surrendering to challenges. Persistence is the key, and with unwavering dedication, your likelihood of success will inevitably increase. Remember, this book serves as your guide, offering strategies to circumvent the pitfalls I encountered and expedite your journey to not only success but also accelerated financial gains.

Engage with the dynamic self-publishing community, thriving across various online platforms such as Facebook groups, YouTube channels, and social media communities. Explore the invaluable insights shared by accomplished authors who have already achieved substantial income through self-published books. Staying informed about the ever-evolving landscape is crucial to avoid falling behind. To ensure you remain updated with the latest information, tips, tricks, and publishing hacks, I encourage you to join my email list by signing up by clicking here or scanning the QR code below. Your connection with this community will be a valuable asset on your self-publishing journey.

In the realm of self-publishing, the path to success is illuminated by the mantra: "write, publish, repeat." The more books you bring to the market, the greater your potential for financial prosperity and the development of a thriving author career. Each publication adds to your growth as a writer, fine-tuning your cover designs and perfecting your overall publishing process. My aim in sharing these invaluable lessons is to pave the way for your success in the world of self-publishing.

To summarize, keep in mind the crucial components of a successful book:

1. Thorough research to identify a profitable keyword.
2. Creation of a well-structured outline.
3. Writing the book.
4. Meticulous editing, either by your hand or a professional editor.
5. Precise formatting, with the option of hiring a formatter.
6. Captivating cover design, which can be crafted by a designer.
7. Uploading your eBook, paperback, and hardcover to KDP.
8. Strategic advertising campaigns for your book.

Now, the moment has arrived for you to embark on your writing journey and seize the opportunity to generate income by self-publishing your books with Amazon KDP!

21

CASE STUDY

You might still be skeptical and be wondering, does this approach genuinely yield results? The answer is a resounding yes, but it requires dedication and consistent effort. My cousin, intrigued by the world of publishing, decided to embark on this journey. I've had around thirty people approach me in the past, expressing their interest once they learn about my endeavors. However, less than five have truly committed to the process. Over time, I've learned to observe and wait before fully engaging, gauging their level of commitment and work ethic.

To my surprise, my cousin proved to be an exception. He diligently worked on his projects, seeking my guidance on a daily basis. This was a refreshing change of pace, and I reciprocated his effort by providing support and answers to his queries. He dedicated dozens of hours each week, and his impressive results are a testament to his hard work.

Below, you'll find a monthly revenue graph from Amazon that showcases his financial progress. Please keep in mind that these figures represent revenue, and to calculate profit, we need to deduct the costs associated with Amazon ads and book covers.

Total revenue from Amazon KDP in USD.

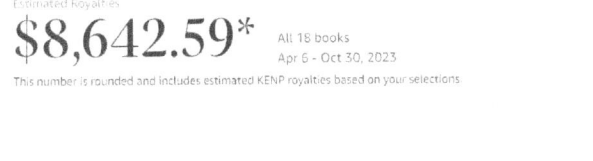

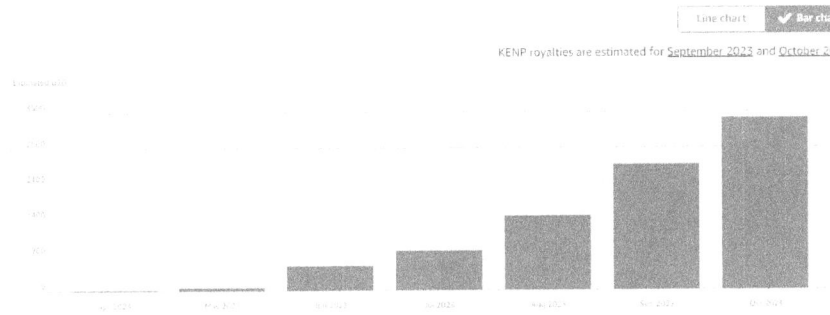

Total amount spent on Amazon Ads in USD.

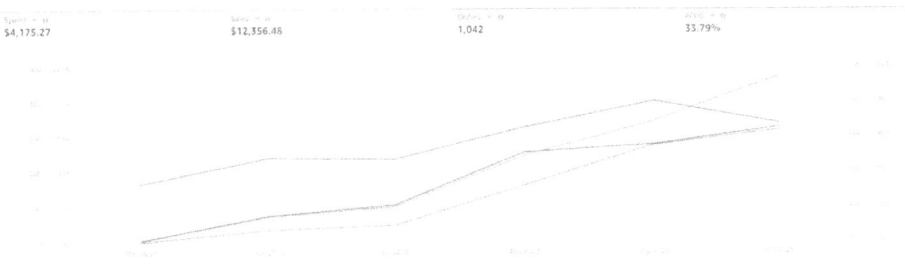

He published 18 books from April to October 2023, spending $50 on each cover, amounting to a total of $900. So, to break down the profit:

$8,642 (revenue) - $4,175 (Amazon ads) - $900 (book covers) = $3,567 (profit).

You might say the $3,567 or $510 per month is a bit underwhelming after seven months of intensive effort invested in this endeavor. However, it's crucial to acknowledge that every journey, especially in the realm of self-publishing, has its own set of challenges and learning curves in the initial stages.

Embarking on this venture requires time and patience, particularly when it comes to mastering the intricacies of Amazon ads, where there's a potential for money to be spent inefficiently. Nevertheless, as proficiency and understanding of the business dynamics improve, the process of creating books becomes more streamlined, advertising expenses are optimized, and revenue generation becomes more substantial.

With a solid grasp of how the business operates now in hand, the potential for quicker book production, more cost-effective ad runs, and an increase in earnings from the existing catalogue of books is significantly enhanced. The initial months of hard work and learning lay down a foundation, making way for smoother operations and increased profitability in the long run.

This opportunity is accessible to anyone willing to invest the necessary effort. Kickstart your journey by creating your first book swiftly, allowing yourself to familiarize with the publishing process firsthand. Once you've done that, download KDSpy to delve into keyword research—this is a pivotal step in this endeavor.

Identifying a profitable keyword is the most important step; without it, the time and resources spent on crafting your book might not yield the desired returns. Following your initial venture, continue the momentum by creating additional books. It's a straightforward process: learn, publish, research, and repeat. By doing so, you're setting yourself up for success in the world of publishing.

22

BONUS: MIDJOURNEY

What Is Midjourney?

Midjourney is an innovative tool powered by artificial intelligence, which stands in the same arena as Chat, albeit with a stark difference in functionality. While Chat is adept at generating textual content, Midjourney is designed to create visual masterpieces, translating prompts into images.

What once took artists days, if not weeks or months, can now be achieved in a matter of seconds with Midjourney. And impressively, its capabilities are improving daily, riding the wave of AI advancements. This is nothing short of extraordinary.

Here's a dive into some unique capabilities and applications of Midjourney:

Breathing Life into Sketches: Midjourney is adept at converting your rough, hand-drawn sketches into digital artworks full of vibrancy and meticulous detail, preserving every subtle nuance.

Instant Mood Boards: Effortlessly create comprehensive mood boards to encapsulate the aesthetic and emotional tone of your projects. Midjourney streamlines this creative process, allowing for a swift compilation and visualization of your conceptual ideas.

From the Simple to the Complex: Experience the creative breadth of Midjourney as it transforms simplistic origami figures into intricate broccoli models, showcasing an expansive spectrum of artistic possibilities.

Crafting Captivating Magazine Cover Art: Elevate your publishing ventures with Midjourney's tools designed to create magazine covers that not only catch the eye but also resonate deeply with your audience.

A Peek into the Microscopic: Embark on a journey to recreate the intricate details found in electron microscope photography, adding a layer of depth and educational value to your scientific or artistic projects.

Conceptualizing New Movies: Discover Midjourney's invaluable contributions to the film industry, assisting in the conceptualization of movies, from character designs to setting the scene, helping to bring your cinematic dreams to reality.

Logo Design: Dive into the world of logo design and learn how Midjourney can aid in creating memorable and impactful brand identities, with practical advice and examples provided every step of the way.

Experimenting with New Art Styles: Push the boundaries of your creativity, experimenting with new art styles using Midjourney, and finding your unique voice in the digital art realm.

Why Is This Relevant in a Book About Publishing?

You might question the relevance of this chapter in a book predominantly about publishing. The connection lies in the unparalleled advantages Midjourney brings to authors and publishers striving to distinguish themselves in a saturated market. This powerful tool allows for the creation of unique and unmatched images that can be utilized to elevate various facets of your book, from cover art to internal illustrations.

By strategically incorporating visually striking and unique imagery, you can captivate potential readers and leave a memorable impression. The distinctive images generated by Midjourney can provide your book with a competitive advantage, ensuring it doesn't just disappear among countless other titles. Utilizing Midjourney is an investment in your book's visual allure, a critical element in capturing attention, sparking interest, and ultimately driving sales. This chapter, while it may initially appear to deviate from the main topic, serves as a guide to utilizing advanced AI-powered tools like Midjourney to amplify your publishing efforts, resulting in a product that is both content-rich and visually stunning.

Why Use Midjourney?

I have harnessed the full potential of Midjourney, employing its sophisticated features to produce images of breathtaking quality, tailored specifically to various book niches. By incorporating these intricate illustrations within each chapter, I offer readers an immersive visual experience that not only augments the book's aesthetic appeal but also provides a welcome diversion from the text.

Even when printed in black and white to maintain cost-effectiveness, the images lose none of their impact or quality. They translate beautifully onto the printed page, captivating readers and leaving a lasting impression. This unique approach has led to an outpouring of positive feedback, with readers expressing their appreciation for the exceptional quality of the images in their reviews.

These visuals serve a purpose beyond beautification; they play a strategic role in distinguishing my brand in a crowded market, helping to carve out a unique identity. The positive reception and the resulting loyal reader base stand as a testament to the effectiveness of integrating unique, high-quality visuals in book publishing. This strategy not only enhances the reader experience but also significantly contributes to establishing a strong, recognizable brand presence.

Pricing

To access the capabilities of Midjourney, you need to visit their official website, midjourney.com, and choose a subscription plan that suits your needs. While it's important to note that the service is not available for free, they do offer a range of pricing options to accommodate different user requirements.

The most basic plan starts at an affordable rate of $10 per month, providing you with ample image generation capacity to meet the visual content needs for your books. This investment is relatively small when considering the unique value and competitive edge that high-quality, customized images can bring to your publications, potentially enhancing your brand's appeal and boosting sales.

All Links

Chat GPT

https://beta.openai.com/

KDP account creation

kdp.amazon.com/signin/

Keyword research software

https://authorpreneuracademy--leadsclick.thrivecart.com/kdspy-v5/

BSR viewer

https://chrome.google.com/webstore/detail/ds-amazon-quick-view/jkompbllimaoekaogchhkmkdogpkhojg

Pen name generator

https://blog.reedsy.com/pen-name-generator/

Paperback cover generator

https://kdp.amazon.com/en_US/cover-calculator

Design software

www.canva.com

Email marketing software

https://app.convertkit.com/users/signup?plan=free-limited&lmref=Lz6sJQ

Amazon advertising

http://advertising.amazon.com

100 Covers

https://100covers.com/

Upwork

https://www.upwork.com/

Fiverr

https://www.fiverr.com/

Midjourney

https://www.midjourney.com/home

If you want all the links on one neatly organized clickable PDF, scan the QR code, enter your email and I'll send it to you!

Thank you!

If you've found the insights in this book helpful, chances are others will too. Why not lend a hand by taking just 30 seconds to leave a review? Your thoughts might be exactly what someone else needs on their self-publishing journey. Thanks for joining me on this adventure!

To leave your review, simply scan the QR code, and it'll take you to the Amazon page where you can easily share your feedback.

www.ingramcontent.com/pod-product-compliance
Lightning Source LLC
Chambersburg PA
CBHW052059110526
44591CB00013B/2281